Hira Aftab / Anam Javeed

A study to explore the extend to which Counter Productive Work Behavior is a shaped by Job Stress

Facts from the Financial Sector of Pakistan

Anchor Academic
Publishing

Aftab, Hira / Javeed, Anam: A study to explore the extend to which Counter Productive Work Behavior is a shaped by Job Stress: Facts from the Financial Sector of Pakistan. Hamburg, Diplomica Verlag GmbH 2013

ISBN: 978-3-95489-042-2
Print: Anchor Academic Publishing, an Imprint of Diplomica® Verlag GmbH, Hamburg, 2013

Bibliographical Information of the German National Library:
The German National Library lists this publication in the German National Bibliography. Detailed bibliographic data can be found at: http://dnb.d-nb.de

The digital publication (eBook) of this work with the ISBN 978-3-95489-542-7 can be purchased on the general market or directly from the publisher.

Work Stress And Counter Work Productive Behavior

Table of Contents

List of Tables

List of Figures

Abbreviations

CWB: Counter-productive Work Behavior

NIOSH: National Institute for Occupational Safety and Health

WHO: World Health Organization

SPSS: Statistical Package for Social Sciences

DFI: development Financial Institutions

SME: Small and Medium Enterprises

SBP: State Bank of Pakistan

OCB: Organizational Citizenship Behavior

Acknowledgement

First of all I want to thank Almighty Allah who has always helped me in every path of life and gave me courage to complete this thesis. I want to thank my parents who have supported me throughout my life.

I also want to thank my supervisor, Miss. Hira Aftab without her sincere guidance it would not have been possible and because of her consistent help and assistance I would be able to complete this research thesis.

Abstract

This research thesis aims to find out the impact of job stress on the counter-productive work behavior (CWB) of employees. Job stress is an important aspect and become a major challenge for the organizations because this job stress became the cause of employee negative behavior.

This research is a causal and a cross sectional one. A sample of 352 employees from the banking sector of Pakistan was used for analysis. Job stress has been measured through different factors and their effect on employee CWB is examined and the study results revealed that the job stress among employees lead them somewhat toward counter-productive work behavior and there is a sufficient positive correlation exist between job stress employee CWB. These results are also consistent with the previous researches that job stress lead the employees towards CWB.

This study reinforces the importance of employees work behavior which is essential for firms to be successful in the current era.

Introduction

Job stress is been an important aspect that become a major challenge for the organizations. Workers who experienced stress have an effect on their work behavior in which they are working. It is understood that employees are not the machines rather they are the most important assets for the organizations as they play a very important role in running the organization effectively and successfully. Better managed employees are more cooperative and serve as assets for an organization but when their stress is ignored by the employer and when the needs of the employees are not catered by the organization properly and stress comes in the organization, then the results are increased absenteeism, cost, low productivity, low motivation and usually legal financial damages which eventually effect the employee work behavior and leads him/her towards the counter-productive work behavior (CWB).

"McGrath (1976) proposed a definition of stress; he defined the stress as a situation in which a person is required to perform the tasks that threatens to exceed the person's ability and resources for meeting it, under conditions where he or she expects a large difference in the rewards from meeting the demand versus not meeting it". (Walonick, 1993)

Job stress has becoming the most essential workplace aspect in the both developed and the developing countries but stress has turn into a massive challenge for employer mainly in developing nations where the employer doesn't provide much weight to the impact of job stress on employee work behavior. There are a numeral workplace factors, called job stressors that make job demanding and complicated for employees in services as well as in other sectors. Other stressors include negative behavior at work, such as absenteeism, increased turnover of employee and employees involved in theft and aggression.

Stress at work have a considerable consequences on employee work behavior but it is made even bad when employee think that they have a little support from their supervisors and boss which inadequately affect the employee behavior inside the organization.

Thesis Statement

The thesis statement is "Impact of job stress on the counter-productive work behavior (CWB) of employees in the financial sector of Pakistan". This thesis would tried to investigate that whether the job stress has an effect on the person who suffered from it or not and if he is suffered than can it lead him toward CWB. To support this thesis different research on it is also found and discussed.

Hypothesis

The main hypothesis is the higher work stress will lead the employee toward CWB means that "higher the work stress, higher will be CWB in employees"

Purpose of the study

The purpose of this study is to find out that whether the job stress has an effect on the work behavior of employees or not, and if is it so, then how the stress damaging the employee and leads him to towards the counter-productive work behavior.

Importance of this study

This study and research is always been a concern for all those who are interested in understanding and knowing the role of job stress on employee behavior in the organization and also to identify that how job stress is been an so important and critical feature in the perspective of the employee behavior.

Objectives

The objectives of this study are as:

- To determine the association between stress at work and employee counter-productive work behavior.
- To what extent the job stress leads the employee to counterwork productive behavior.

Significance

Over the years stress at work has become one of the most extensively studied constructs in organizations. This study primarily aims to illustrate the relationship between work stress and its impact on employee work behavior. "In work stress is so aversive to employees that they will try to avoid it by withdrawing either psychologically (disinterest or lack of involvement in the work etc.), physically (frequent late coming, absenteeism, laziness etc.) or by leaving the job entirely". (Muhammad Mansoor; Sabtain Fida; Saima Nasir; Zubair Ahmad., 2011)

Background

Work Stress

"Since 1956, when stress was introduced into the American vernacular, the concept has been whole heartedly embraced by popular culture. Today, the cultural connotations of stress often overpower its actual definition. By 1956, Selye had added to the developing ideas about stress by putting forward a three stage process. According to him, stress is a phenomenon in response to some external stressor we first react by mobilizing our physical resources to deal with or escape from the stressor. The second stage, called 'resistance', involves ways of coping with the alarm stage by trying to reverse it. Thirdly, the stage of 'exhaustion' occurs if an individual is repeatedly exposed to the stressor and is unable to escape. Over the 30 years there are different researchers and different researches on it." (Kennard, 2008)

CWB

"The domain of counter productive work behavior (CWB) is quite abroad prior to the early 1980 there was a considerable amount of research on individual counter productive behaviors in the workplace such as employee theft, sabotage, slow and sloppy performance, tardiness and absenteeism. However due to lack of accepted theory or framework for looking at such behaviors, these studies were each seen as an investigation into a specific type of behavior rather than an effort to explore CWB in a more general sense. Robinson and Greenberg in 1998 reviewed a wide variety of definitions on the counterproductive work behavior that are found in the literature. However the most recent definition was been given by De Vore (2001) as: any intentional behavior on the part of an organization member viewed by the organization as contrary to its legitimate interests. This definition is considered the most relevant and important because with this definition of CWB the focus is on the behavior itself rather than on the results and consequences of the behaviors." (Gruys & Sackett, 2003)

Banking Sector of Pakistan

"A sound and well functioning financial sector is essential to support economic growth of a country. Pakistan possess a wide range of financial institutions; commercial banks, specialized banks, national savings schemes, insurance companies, DFI's, investment banks, stock exchanges, corporate brokerage houses, leasing companies, discount houses, microfinance institutions, SME's and Islamic banks. They offer a whole range of products and services both on the assets and liabilities side. Pakistani banking sector has witnessed drastic changes over a period of 63 years. Today, the Banking sector of Pakistan is playing pivotal role in the growth of country's economy. In accordance with the State Bank of Pakistan Act, the banking system of Pakistan is a two-tier system including the State Bank of Pakistan (SBP), commercial banks, specialized banks, Development Finance Institutions (DFIs), Microfinance banks and Islamic banks. As of June 2010, the banking sector comprised 36 commercial banks (including 25 local private banks, 4 public sector commercial banks and 7 foreign banks) and 4 specialized banks with a total number of 9,087 branches throughout the country. Among the banks, there are 6 fully fledged Islamic banks as at end of June 2010." (Pervez, 25th feb, 2011)

Literature Review

There are several studies that have tried to determine the effect of job stress on employee behavior in the organization.

Variables

There are two variables in the study which is work stress and employee work counter-productive work behavior and there are many researches that have been done in the area of work stress.

Stress

Hans Selye view in 1956 about the stress was "stress isn't necessarily something bad – it all depends on how you take it. The stress of exhilarating, creative successful work is beneficial, while that of failure, humiliation or infection is detrimental." (Sanvee, 2009)

"In the words of Richard S Lazarus, basically stress is a feeling that is experienced when a person started thinking that the demands exceeds the personal and social resources the individual is able to mobilize."

Work Stress

"Work-related stress occurs when one's job demands are incompatible or mismatched with the mental regulation processes, such as information processing, planning, and movement execution". (Greiner, 1998)

In the words of Westman "Job stress arises when demand of job exceed abilities, while job-related strains are responses or outcomes resulting from the experience of stress." (Westman, 2005)

Stress at workplace has a severe safety and healthiness hazards that can have destructive effects. Stress is a major cause of psychosocial sickness; such as tense muscles can aggravate ergonomic injuries. The workers who experienced stress can be more vulnerable to injury, health and disease. (Enough Workplace Stress: Organizing for Change, 2003)

Generally it is believed that some stress has positive effects on individuals which is referred to as "Challenge or Positive Stress" but when stress goes beyond the amount which you are not been able to handle then both physical and mental alterations may arise. Work related stress then arise as a result of differences between employee job demands and an employee amount of control over gathering these demands which can cause a harmful impact on employee physical and emotional responses. In short the amalgamation of very high demands in a job and the employee low amount of control over the situation is a major cause of stress. Stress at workplace can be come from multiple events or can be from single events and it has a huge impact on employers and employees alike. According to "Canadian Mental Association" job redundancy. Layoff fears in an economy which is uncertain, excessive workload due to staff cutbacks are the major negative stressors and the employees who are starting to feel the pressure to perform get involved in a negative and downward spiral of highly increasing efforts to meet increased expectations with no increase in job satisfaction. The unyielding requirements to work at optimum performance leads to the increase in toll in employee job dissatisfaction, turnover of employees, reduced efficiency and employee illness. Absenteeism, lack of involvement, lack of participation in decision making, apathy and indifference, lack of creativity or motivation are all by-products of the workplace which is over stressed. (Workplace Stress - General, 2008)

The journal article on "Stressful work, job satisfaction, intention to leave and organization citizenship behavior: examining the mediating role of job satisfaction" was conducted to examine the relationship between job stress, employee intention to leave means employee turnover and OCB. In the research it is found that increased stressful work and stressful environment increased the employee desire to leave the organization so the work stress was correlated positively with employee intention to leave the employer or negatively correlated with OCB and that job dissatisfaction increases in employees who experienced work stress. This job dissatisfaction among employees motivating them to increase absenteeism and to quit the organization. Stress can cause health problems for employees and loss of profits for employers. The results found in this study are consistent with the previous researches that stressful work causes job dissatisfaction among employees. Finally the results of this study proved that unsatisfactory employment act as a bridge between employee work stress and his intention to leave the employer. (Paillé, Stressful Work, Citizenship Behaviour and Intention to Leave the Organization in a High Turnover Environment: Examining the Mediating Role of Job Satisfaction., 2011).

The research paper on "Impact of job stress on employee job satisfaction" investigated the effects of job stress on employee job satisfaction. In this paper a sample of 134 employees from the telecom sector of Pakistan. The job stress has been measured by three important dimensions which are work conflicts, employee workload and physical environment. The study revealed that all the three factors of job stress effect the job satisfaction of employee negatively. The study results also been supported by the prior studies results that employee who feel excessive stress found their job dissatisfying. It is also found in this study that the subjects who have experienced more stress by the factors including work conflict, excessive workload and physical environment was found to be less satisfying as compared to those employees who experienced less stress. (Mansoor, Muhammad; Fida, Sabtain; Nasir, Saima; Ahmad, Zubair, 2004).

There is another study to examine that whether the organizational stressor variables had contributing to manager's job stress or not. In this study sample of 285 respondents were taken. The organizational variables taken in this study were role conflict, no advancement opportunities for employees, extreme work load and unfavorable workplace environment. The regression analysis were done on this and the results revealed that out of all organizational stressors, three of the stressors which are role conflict, no advancement for opportunities and work environment were been the major cause of job stress among managers. (Aizzat Mohd Nasurdin; T. Ramayah; S. Kemaresan).

According to different surveys conducted by "American Psychological Association (2008)" more than half of the respondents reported that stress is a significant reason of their poor performance and almost three of half reported that stress is a major cause of their bad health. Another survey study conducted by "Multi employer, multi-site employee" exposed that employees who have high level of stress, their health expenditures were 46% higher as compared to the employees with no stress. Job stress costed US economy about 300 billion a year in the form of employee absenteeism, low employee productivity, employee turnover and medical and insurance costs. (Research roundup: Work stress, 2010)

Figure 1: What Workers say about stress on job

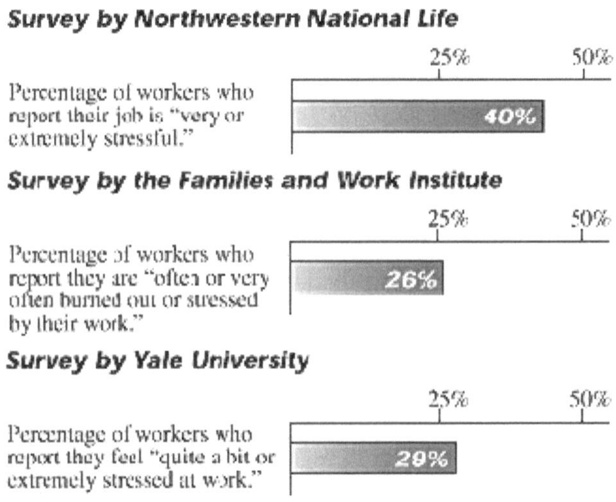

"According to this report workers at different places do report that they have to face stress and do report that their job is extremely stressful". (NIOSH: stress at work, 2010)

According to different researches, "Job stress has become a common and costly problem in the American workplace, leaving few workers unaffected. For example, studies report the following:"

- "Almost one-fourth of employees in different organizations view their jobs as the number one stressor in their lives."

-Northwestern National Life

- "Almost three-fourths of employees in different organizations believe they have more on-the-job stress than a generation ago."

-Princeton Survey Research Associates

Mismatch with the organization in the way that employees are given no rights in decision making were found out to be the main reason of work stress as well as if employees does not have any control over work environment, personality characteristics and unclear rules and policies and unclear roles effect employee performance. (Meneze, 2005).

The data of **"Bureau of Labor Statistics"** showed that stress and anxiety are the major causes of workers absenteeism and that the workers who take their time off due to stress or anxiety or any other related problem will not be on a job for about 20 days. (NIOSH - U.S. Department of Health and Services.)

Workplace stress effect employees over the past many years. This workplace stress occurs due to increased workload and clients demands. The increased level of stress in employees affects not only the employee health but also ends up costing the economy in the shape of employee absenteeism, employee loss of productivity and turnover. The clients are also decreasing because the more stressed the workers is feeling, the less likely they are been able to perform their jobs at full potential. (Klink & al., Work-related Stress in Division of Youth and Family Caseworkers: Determining Whether a Cognitive Behavioral Intervention Will Decrease Stress., 2001).

Stress is often a end-product of poor boss attitude and poor workplace environment and have a serious effect on organizational productivity and growth. Therefore organizations that have effective stress management programs, talk on regular basis with their workers and have efficient system, procedures and policies to deal with employee stress related issues like employee absence and workplace discipline are much more able to avoid stress situations and to cope up with employee problems as they arise. (Working together to reduce stress at work. A guide for employees., 2008)

The work-related stress occur due to "Poor organization design" such as poor inappropriate work systems or workplace environment, improper job alienation and the way we manage it, and "Poor work designs" such as no employee participation in decision making and their lack of control over work processes, by poor management and no support from boss, colleagues and supervisors. Employees feel less stressed when their job and work demands matched with their knowledge and abilities and they have a right to participate in decision making and proper support is received from all the supervisors and colleagues. (World Health Organization.)

The Work Stress effects on individuals

According to the Health and Safety Executive, "prolonged work-related stress can lead to: poor mental health; heart disease; back pains, gastrointestinal disturbances and miscellaneous minor illnesses including trouble with gums or mouth and toothache, shortness of breath, dizziness, earache, swollen ankles, rashes or itches and headaches; and an increase in unhelpful health behavior such as missing breakfast, drinking too much alcohol and smoking." (Stress survey, 2001) Work-related stress is currently the second most key work-related health trouble in the UK. According to Stress survey 2001 the core or vital foundation of job stress with their percentages are as

Figure 2: Effects of stress

Effects Of Stress	**Respondents %**
Low energy/tiredness	73
Difficulty relaxing	61
Been very irritable	61
Warning a lot	55
Lost interest in things	47
Difficulty in concentrating	43
Felt hopeless/depressed	37
Lost confidence in myself	33
Had to take prescribed drugs or mediation	16
Lost weight due to poor appetite	9

These are the impact of stress on persons in a European culture. (Stress survey, 2001)

Work Stress Causes

Stress can be occurring from several reasons, starting from excessively work to mal-treatment or hostility. Terrible management and extreme workloads came out undoubtedly as the main two problems leading to stress in organizations. According to Stress survey 2001 the foremost or central causes of job stress with their percentages are as. (Stress survey, 2001)

Figure 3: Causes of Stress

Causes Of Stress	Respondents %
Bad management	44
Excessive workloads	42
Staff shortages	20
No job security	17
Boring work	16
Long hours	13
Bullying	11
Lack of control	11
Hazardous conditions	9
Lack of rest breaks	7
Others	5
Discrimination	4
Threat of violence	2
Poor children facilities	1

Fortunately, work stress explorations have been comprehensive in the recent years. But putting out-of-the-way all this attentiveness, vagueness remain the major cause of job stress. (Stress At Work, 2010)

Employee Counter-Productive work Behavior (CWB)

Counterproductive workplace behavior (CWB) has turn into a progressively accepted issue of learning between researchers. "Counter-productive work behavior (CWB) is any intentional behavior on the part of an organization member, viewed by the organization as contrary to its legitimate interests". (Gruys & Sakett, 2003)

A study on "Job Stressors, Negative Affectivity and Counter-Productive Work Behavior (CWB)" tried to investigate the relationship between job stressors and their effect on employee counter-productive work behavior (CWB) keeping in view the role of negative affectivity. The results show incivility, poor organizational environment and conflicts among employees were negatively correlated with employee job satisfaction and lead him toward the counter-productive work behavior (CWB). The results of this study are consistent with the previous studies showing a relationship between job stress and employee counter-productive work behavior (CWB). The results also showed that the individuals who have higher negative affectivity with organizations are more going towards the counter-productive work behaviors than for individuals who are low in negative affectivity. This shows that being subjected to incivility could aggravate an individual to go towards negative attitude and as a result employees are engaged in retaliatory acts such as CWB. Furthermore this study also shows that individuals who engaged in counter-productive work behaviors (CWB) would be the cause of creating a workplace incivility. (Penney & Spector, 2005).

Another study on "Effect of job stress on health, personal and work behavior of nurses in public hospitals in Ibadan Metropolis, Nigeria" tried to find out the relationship between job stresses on nurses and its effect on their health and their work behavior which mainly include their behavior with patients. The results showed that the job stress is the major cause of nurse's bad health and cause great health problems for them. Job stress is negatively associated with their work behavior and an increased level of stress provokes them to engage in behaviors such as absenteeism, withdrawal and aggressive or impolite behavior with patients. (Mojoyinola, J. K., 2008) .

According to one of the survey conducted by "CCH Inc" revealed that stress is one of the major causes of unscheduled absences from work. Employee absences or absenteeism is defend as the work time missed by an employee and the survey results show that stress related illnesses and health problems cause 70% of job absenteeism. (Kim, Sorhaindo, & Garman, 2006)

The research on "Impact of job stress on employee productivity, performance and turnover" said that stress is a universal element and the persons from nearly all aspects of life have to face it. Today stress management issues are critically analyzed by the employees that lead them towards low job satisfaction and high turnover. The survey results shown that overall sample is facing stress because of low acceptance for work done by the top management, rigid organizational structure, lack of support from supervisors and colleagues and unclear roles are the main causes of increasing stress levels in employees which ultimately effect their job performance negatively and lead them toward leaving the organization. (Imtiaz & Ahmad, 2009).

Another study on "The role of personality, occupation and organization in understanding the relationship between job stress, performance and absenteeism" tried to examine the relationship between stress with important behavioral perspective of employee i.e. absenteeism keeping in view the role played by personality and occupation. The results of this study indicated that job stress are the major reason of increased absenteeism in employees resulting poor employee performance and personalities was found to have a major effect on employee performance. (Arsenault & Dolan, 1983)

"St. Paul's report indicated that interpersonal demands on employees are increasing. This in itself creates tremendous stress. Interpersonal demands due to working with team members and supervisors were the most significant cause of stress burnout. Thus, in today's workplace, we have people who are already under stress from a variety of causes put into an interpersonal context that, by its nature, is very stressful. Being already stressed-out, they are less likely to respond appropriately and constructively, further heightening the likelihood they will find such a demanding interpersonal context even more difficult and depleting." (Lee, 1997)

The ratio of stress in employees in organizations is increasing at disturbing rate. All the studies mentioned above also show that stress result in high absenteeism, turnover and poor performance. That's why it is very imperative to consider job stress as an essential and critical factor in organizations from the employee behavioral perspective.

Gap Analysis of Job Stress and Employee CWB

Past Researches	Population	Results	Area	Conclusion
Work Motivation, Job Stress & Employee Well-being.	The target population is home interviewed 300 working adults living in Kaohsiung city, Taiwan.	Results show that conflicts at work are the main cause of anxiety or stress. Motivation also positively correlated with social support from all the sources and job satisfaction.	Management	The main aim of this study is to find out relationship between motivation, stress and employee well-being. Of all the factors like depression and anxiety. Stress is strongly positively correlated with anxiety. Work motivation also has an effect on employee well-being.
Impact of stress on employee productivity, performance and turnover.	The target samples are the medical and house officers working in both the public and private hospitals of Rawalpindi and Islamabad.	Stress was significantly negatively correlated with job performance. Stress is caused by low admin support, lack of acceptance for work done and inadequate work environment effect employee productivity and performance negatively.	Management	On the basis of survey results it is concluded that overall sample has faces low acceptance for work done, high unpredictability, low admin support and inadequate monetary rewards are the main causes of rising stress level in the sample which ultimately affects their job performance negatively.

Effect of job stress on health, personal and work behavior of nurses.	The participants of the study are nurses working in public hospitals in Ibadan, Nigeria.	The results revealed that stress is a major cause of bad behavior of nurses causing physical or mental problems. The results also showed that 85% of the nurses experienced stress due to excessive workload, no promotion and poor salary.	Management	The study investigated the effect of job stress on physical mental and work behavior of nurses. The results collected through questionnaires shows the presence of stress among nurses make them to engage in withdrawal, displaced or hostile behavior with the patients.
Impact of job stress on employee job satisfaction.	The sample of this study consists of 134 employees from telecom sector of Pakistan.	The results supporting the hypothesis and prior studies that job stress Is negatively correlated with employee job satisfaction. Subjects were found to face more stress in the form of workload, role conflict and physical environment.	Management	This research paper examines the impact of job stress on employee job satisfaction. It is concluded that Individuals under stress tend to find their job less satisfying. Due to intense competition in telecom sector organizations are exerting more pressure on employees to compete that decreases their job satisfaction.
Organiza-	Participants in	The job stress is explained by var-		It was concluded that

tional stressors and job stress among managers: The moderating role of neuroticism.	this study were managers from 20 randomly selected local and foreign electronic firms located in Malaysia.	ious organizational variables. It is found that three of five variables which are blocked career, work overload and conflict have a positive relationship with job stress and moderating variable neuroticism have a significant interaction with the organizational stressors.	Management	the purpose of the current study was two-fold, first to determine the effect of organizational stressors on job stress among managers and to test whether these relationships vary according to the level of neuroticism. The regression results shows three out of five variables had positive relationship with job stress.
Occupational stress and its effect on job performance.	The study consisted of house officers working in Ayub Teaching Hospital, Abbotabad.	The analysis shows strong support that there is an inverse relationship between job stress and job performance indicating that a high job stress in house officers resulting in low job performance.	Management	The principle purpose of this study was to find out the stress performance relationship. The data demonstrates the strong support for hypothesis. Lacks of resources and communication have contributed to increased stress in the house officers which contribute to lower job performance.
Stressful work, citizenship be-	The participants are the	The result indicates that while stress was nega-		In this study it is concluded that increased stressful work increased

havior and intention to leave the organization: Examining the mediating role of job satisfaction.	engineers graduated from French Engineering School.	tively related to job satisfaction it was not significantly related to OCB. Job satisfaction was negatively related to intention to leave and positively related to OCB.	Management	the employee desire to leave the organization. Work stress was negatively correlated with OCB and that job dissatisfaction increases in employees who experienced work stress motivating them to increase absenteeism and to quit the organization.
Job stress, incivility and CWB: The moderating role of negative affectivity.	The target sample in this study was employed persons taking courses at public university in South Eastern US.	The results show incivility, poor organizational environment and conflicts among employees reduced employee job satisfaction and lead him toward (CWB) and the individuals who have higher negative affectivity with organizations are more going towards (CWB).	Management	The study concluded that employees subjected to job stress and incivility goes towards negative attitude and as a result employees are engaged in retaliatory acts such as CWB. Furthermore this study also shows that individuals who engaged in counter-productive work behaviors (CWB) due to increased stress would be the cause of creating a workplace incivility.
The role of personality, occupation in understanding the relationship between job stress, performance and absen-	The study includes 1200 employees from 8 hospitals.	The results of this study indicated that job stress are the major reason of increased absenteeism in employees resulting poor employee performance and personalities was	Management	The overall conclusion from the study is that job stress are positively correlated with employees increased absenteeism and negatively correlated with employee performance. The results also revealed that blue-collar employees show a significant de-

teeism.		found to have a major effect on employee performance.		crease in absenteeism when they deal with job content stress.
Leadership style and link with CWB.	Participants were 172 employees from Tampa Bay Area, Florida.	This study shows that poor leadership style act as a stressor that leads the employee to CWB.	Management	The study explains the inclusion of leadership style as a stressor in job stress and CWB and concluded that good leaders are those who respond to employee problems quickly.

In the light of the few past researches that I have been studied or mentioned above in the summary of past researches, this research thesis is contributing to the previous researches in many ways as no research has been conducted purely on "The impact of job stress on the counter-productive work behavior of employees". Many researches have been done on "The impact of work stress on employee performance and behavior" but this research focus mainly on the counter-productive work behavior of employee occur due to stress.

Furthermore, no past research had been done on the banking sector of Pakistan whereas this research targets the banking sector of Pakistan.

Research Methodology

Purpose of study

The purpose of this study is to find out the relationship between job stress and employee behavior, how the job stress will direct the employee towards counter-productive work behavior. It is an explanatory study because it gives a complete study on the impact of job stress on employee behavior.

Research Design

This research is a basic and causal research because in this we are tried to determine the causes of job stress on employees and in addition to that this research is a cross sectional study.

Time Dimension

This study is a cross sectional one as it is used questionnaire for collecting the data and is conducted at one point in time.

Data Collection Methods

The data is collected through questionnaire for investigating the impact of job stress on employee counter-productive work behavior from different banks of Lahore. The questionnaire will be distributed among middle level management of different banks having a designation of AVP, OG-I, OG-II and OG-III.

Questionnaire

The questionnaire contains three main parts and total 71 items. The first part is the demographics, second part is on job stress containing 25 questions to access the stress among employees and third part is on employee CWB containing 28 questions. The items were measured using Likert scale.

Pilot Testing

Before going to the actual phase of questionnaire filling, the pilot testing is been done. In this 5 questionnaires was distributed to check the validity and errors in the questions.

Sample Frame

The target population in this study will be the middle level managers working in different banks. So, the target population is basically from the banking sector.

Sample Size

The sample size in this study will be of 352 employees. Our representative sample is the middle level of employees from different banks.

Unit of Analysis

The unit of analysis in our research is the middle level management working in banks.

Sampling Procedure

For sampling probability sampling technique is used to collect data. The data is been collected by the questionnaire from randomly selected 352 middle level managers working in different banks of Lahore. The obtained data is analyzed through SPSS version 17. The statistical methods involved those of descriptive statistics of Independent Variable of Stress and dependent variable CWB. Inferential statistics (Pearson Correlation &

Linear Regression) defines the relationship between the independent and dependent variables.

Theoretical Framework

Independent Variable: Job Stress.

Dependent Variable: Employee counter-productive work behavior (CWB) in the organization.

Hypothesis

1. There will be a significant effect of job stress on the counter-productive work behavior of employees.
2. The significant effect of job stress will lead the employee towards CWB

Explanation

The hypothesis is measurable and has a significant importance because job stress has a significant negative impact on employees as "stress is a situation in which employee feel pressure for the work it won't be able to do because of many factors". The stress has a various harmful physical, emotional and environmental responses which have a very harmful effect on employees like Fatigue or Illness, nervousness, memory problems, more time to complete task, unclear role in organization, seeing only negative, short temper, unfair performance evaluation system, increased no. of errors and decreased devotion for the organization in which they work for. These all factors certainly will give rise to employee negative work behavior and provoke him to engage in counter-productive work behavior

On the other hand, CWB has also been a growing discussion for many years. Employees behavior has an huge impact on organizations. The major reason for growing interest in job stress and employee CWB is unfortunately due to its common presence in employees and organizations.

Tremendous job stress makes the employees less engage in work and as a result organizations suffer loss in productivity and increased employees health and insurance costs. This increased costs and loss in productivity costing the organization and even the whole economy making the employee less satisfied and this job dissatisfaction along with all the job stressors lead the employee toward counter-productive work behavior (CWB).

By amalgamating both the job stress and CWB, the old literature also explained and suggests that counter-productive work behavior are the negative behaviors that occur due to a response to various job stressors at work. As a result many researchers view a variety of job stressors of extreme importance and seen as a threat for organizations and employees negative behavior that also increases the anger and anxiety among employees. Today all literature and researches provide findings that showed job stress is become a major reason for organizations retaliatory behavior and workplace deviance and the main reason behind all these findings is job dissatisfaction which motivating the individuals to increased absenteeism, aggressive behavior and CWB.

Operationalization of Variables

In this research there are two variables which is job stress and counter-productive work behavior (CWB).

Variable 1: Job Stress

Conceptual definition

"Job stress occurs when one's job demands are incompatible or mismatched with the mental regulation processes, such as information processing, planning, and movement execution. (Greiner, 1998)"

Operational definition

Job stress is measured against the responses of twenty five questions that the individual enter on the questionnaire observing for the period of particular length.

Dimensions of Job Stress

The dimensions of job stress are:

- Stressful physical response
- Stressful emotional response
- Stressful environmental response

Elements

Stressful physical response

- ❖ Nervousness or Memory problems

Statements

My job requires huge deal of attention beyond my job's range.

My job requires me to remember many different things.

- ❖ Excessive workload

Statements

I have excessive workload than normal work.

Always there is a bundle of tasks for me to be undertaken

- ❖ More time to complete a task

Statements

Due to excessive workload, I could not finish my work during the normal work day.

Most of the time I am forced to work more.

- ❖ Role in organization

Statements

My job responsibilities and role in the organization are not clear.

- ❖ Poor communication

Statements

There is a poor communication between my staff members and different departments.

There are conflicts between staff members.

Stressful emotional response

- Seeing only negative

Statements

I have uncomfortable workplace

My work place is Boring and dull.

- Opportunities of promotion

Statements

There are no opportunities of advancement in my organization.

- Affection

Statements

I do not receive any appreciation when my work is really good.

- Unfair performance evaluation system

Statements

There is unfair performance evaluation system in our organization.

I am not satisfied with my salary and rewards this is not what I deserve

- ❖ No emotional attachment

Statement

I don't feel any kind of emotional attachment with my work

Stressful environmental response

- ❖ Workplace environment

Statements

The level of noise in the area in which I work is high.

My work area is extremely crowded.

- ❖ Job requirements

Statements

Due to technological change, it is difficult for me to deal with problems.

Due to age factor, it is not easy for me to cope with changes.

- ❖ Shout from boss

Statements

My boss shouts at me

My boss pressurizes me to work more than what I am assigned to do

- ❖ Leg Pulling

Statements

I experience leg pulling behavior from my colleagues

- ❖ Working hours

Statements

At my work place there is long working hours

There is so much pressure of work that I have to work overtime even on the weekends

Variable 2: CWB

Conceptual definition

"Counter-productive work behavior (CWB) is any intentional behavior on the part of an organization member, viewed by the organization as contrary to its legitimate interests". (Gruys & Sakett, 2003)

Operational definition

CWB can be measured against the scores of the responses an individual given in the questionnaire for an observation period of particular length.

Dimensions of CWB

- ❖ Absenteeism
- ❖ Workplace Deviance
- ❖ Aggression
- ❖ Theft

Elements

Absenteeism

- ❖ Come late to work

Statements

Came to work late without permission

- ❖ Stayed at home

Statements

Stayed home to avoid work and said you were sick when you weren't.

- ❖ Take a longer break

Statements

Taken a longer break than you were allowed to take

- ❖ Left work earlier

Statements

Left work earlier than you were allowed to

Workplace Deviance

- ❖ Wasted material / supplies

Statements

Purposely wasted materials/supplies available in my organization

- ❖ Damaged equipment

Statements

Purposely damaged equipment or property of my organization

- ❖ Work incorrectly

Statements

Purposely did the work assigned to you incorrectly

- ❖ Worked slowly

Statements

Purposely worked slowly when things needed to get done

- ❖ Don't follow

Statements

Purposely don't follow the instructions

Aggression

- ❖ Been nasty or rude

Statements

Been nasty or rude to a client or customer

Said something to someone at work to make them feel bad

- ❖ Insulting behavior

Statements

Insulted someone about their job performance

Insulted or made fun of someone at work

- ❖ Made fun of others

Statements

Made fun of someone's personal life

- ❖ Ignored or blamed someone

Statements

Ignored someone at work

Blamed someone at work for error you made

- ❖ Abusive behavior

Statements

Verbally abused someone at work

- ❖ Threatening someone

Statements

Threatened someone at work with violence

Threatened someone at work, but not physically

Hit or pushed someone at work.

Theft

- ❖ Stole something

Statements

Stolen something belonging to your colleagues at work

Stole something belonging to someone at work

- ❖ Took money or supplies

Statements

Took supplies or tools home without permission

Took money from your employer without permission

Put in to be paid for more hours than you worked

- ❖ Look at someone's property

Statements

Looked at someone at work's private mail/property without permission.

Analysis

Reliability tests

Reliability test of job stress

Table 1

Cronbach's Alpha	N of Items
.938	25

The chronbach alpha for 25 items of job stress is 0.938 showing high internal consistency. The chronbach score was 0.938 > 0.70. This means that there are sufficient questions in questionnaire to check job stress among respondents.

Reliability test of employee CWB

Table 2

Cronbach's Alpha	N of Items
.963	28

The chronbach alpha for 28 items of impact of job stress on employees CWB is 0.963 showing high internal consistency. The chronbach score was 0.963 > 0.70. This means that there are sufficient questions in questionnaire to check impact of job stress on employees involved in counter –productive work behavior.

Reliability test of questionnaire

Table 3

Cronbach's Alpha	**N of Items**
.942	71

The chronbach alpha score for the questionnaire is 0.942. It means that our questionnaire is 94.2% reliable.

Descriptive Statistics

Frequency and graphical presentation of demographical variables

Gender

Table 4

	Fre-quency	Percent	Cumulative Percent
Male	276	78.4	78.4
Female	76	21.6	100.0
Total	352	100.0	

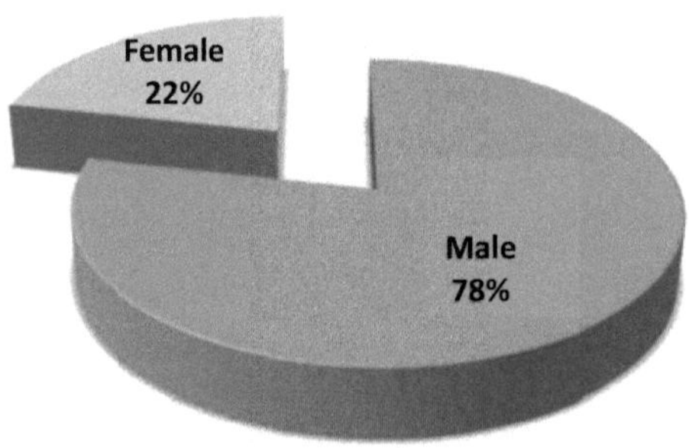

In the research there are total 352 respondents out of which 276 are the males which comprise of 78.4% of total population and just 76 females which made 21.6% of the total population.

Age

Table 5

	Frequency	Percent	Cumulative Percent
Under 26	67	19.0	19.0
26-35	126	35.8	54.8
36-45	92	26.1	81.0
46-55	46	13.1	94.0
56+	21	6.0	100.0
Total	352	100.0	

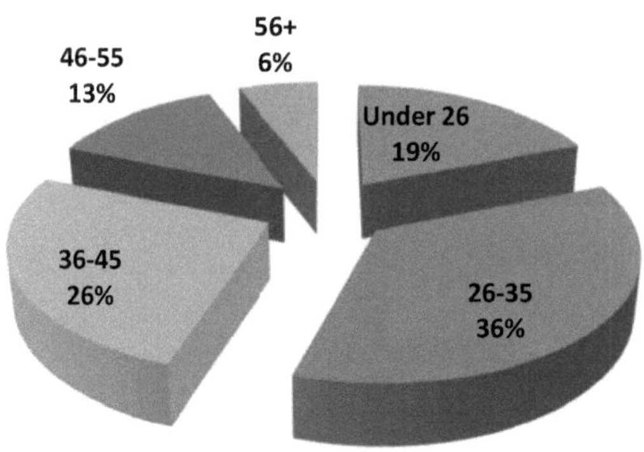

In the research there are 67 respondents who are under 26 years of age, 126 individuals comprising of 36% are from 26-35 years age group, 26% respondents are from 36-45 years age, 13% are from 46-55 years age and the rest of 6% are from 56+ age group.

The highest percentage of sample is 36% from 26-35 years age group.

Monthly Salary

Table 6

	Fre-quency	Percent	Cumulative Percent
Less than 25,000	76	21.6	21.6
25,000-40,000	128	36.4	58.0
40,001-55,000	75	21.3	79.3
55,001-70,000	41	11.6	90.9
More than 70,000	32	9.1	100.0
Total	352	100.0	

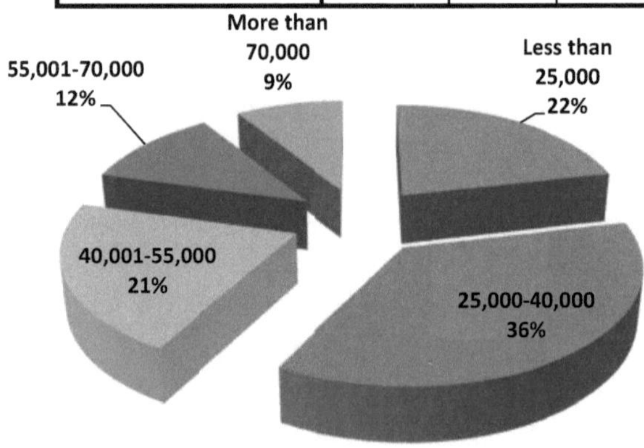

In the monthly salary, there are 76 individuals consist of 21.6% who get the monthly salary less than 25,000, 36% came in the 25,000-40,000, 21% came in the 40,000-

55,000, 12% came in the 55,000-70,000 and the 9% individuals came in the more than 70,000 monthly salary range.

The highest percentage is 36% of the individuals who are taking monthly salary in 25,000-40,000 salary bracket.

Doing this job for

Table 7

	Frequency	Percent	Cumulative Percent
Few months less than 1 year	33	9.4	9.4
1-3 years	80	22.7	32.1
3-6 years	85	24.1	56.3
6-9 years	53	15.1	71.3
More than 9 years	101	28.7	100.0
Total	352	100.0	

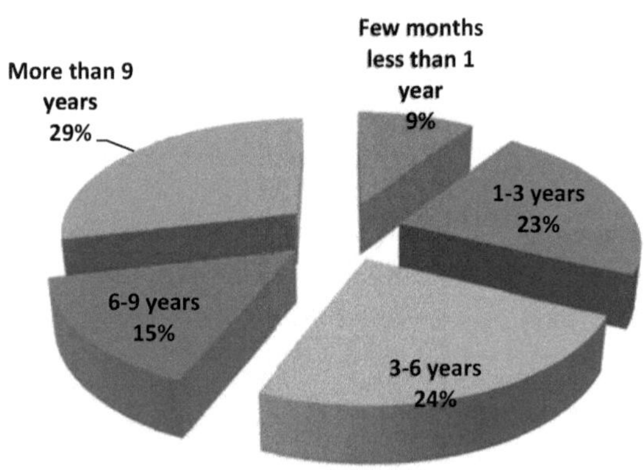

Table 7 shows the number of years of total sample current job that they are doing and the results shows that there are 33 respondents who are just 9.4% of the total population that are doing job for few months less than 1 year, whereas there are 80 individuals

(22.7%) who are doing their jobs for 1-3 years, 24% are on their job for 3-6 years, 15% are doing their current jobs for 6-9 years and the 29% respondents are on their jobs for more than 9 years.

Nature of job

Table 8

	Frequency	Percent	Cumulative Percent
You have to work in this office	242	68.8	68.8
You have a field job	30	8.5	77.3
Both office and field job	80	22.7	100.0
Total	352	100.0	

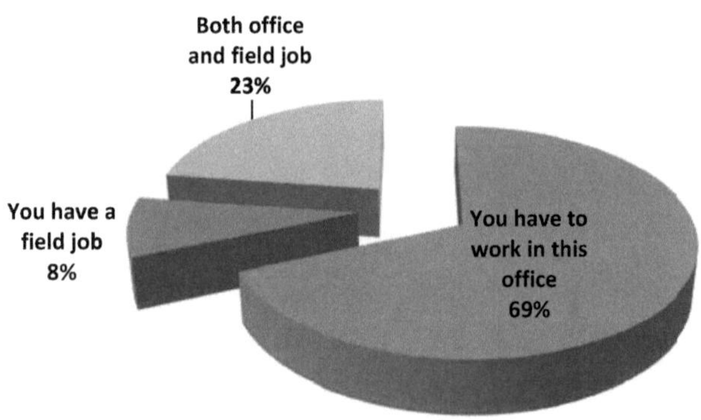

In the nature of job, there are 242 individuals comprising of 68.8% of the total population who are doing the jobs in their offices only, 8% have field jobs and the remaining 23% have both office and field job.

The highest percentage 68.8% is of the individuals who are saying that they have to work in office.

Total Professional Experience

Table 9

	Frequency	Percent	Cumulative Percent
Few months less than 1 year	25	7.1	7.1
1-3 years	74	21.0	28.1
3-6 years	75	21.3	49.4
6-9 years	46	13.1	62.5
More than 9 years	132	37.5	100.0
Total	352	100.0	

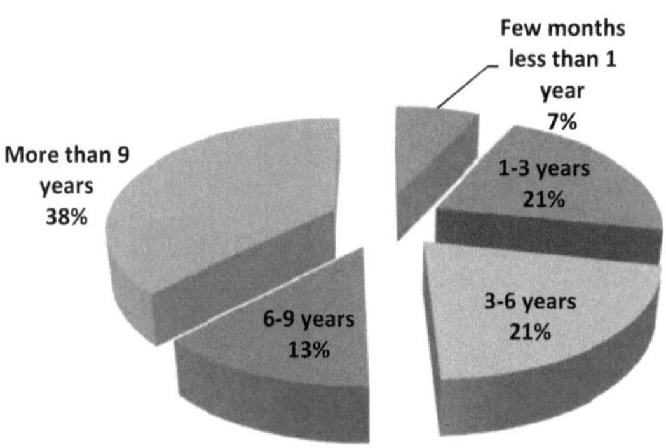

In the total period of professional experience, there are just 7% respondents who have the total professional experience of less than a year, 74 individuals (21%) have professional experience of 1-3 years, 21% have professional experience of 3-6 years, 13%

have professional experience of 6-9 years and the remaining 132 respondents consist of 38% have the total professional experience of more than 9 years.

So, the highest percentage is of the individuals who have total professional experience of more than 9 years.

Number of Jobs Switched

Table 10

	Frequency	Percent	Cumulative Percent
No its my first job	195	55.4	55.4
Less than 2	118	33.5	88.9
Less than 4	26	7.4	96.3
Less than 6	5	1.4	97.7
More than 6	8	2.3	100.0
Total	352	100.0	

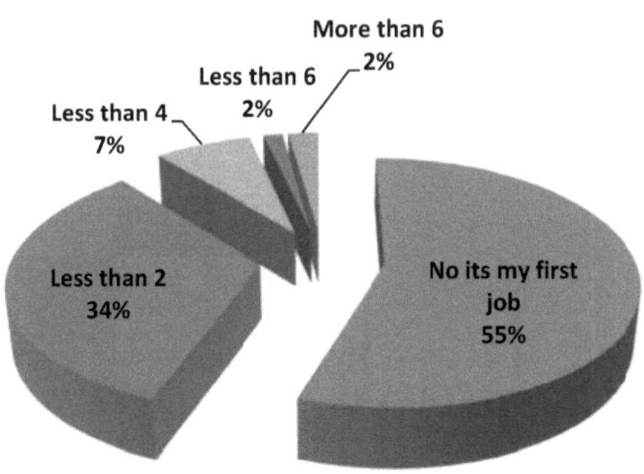

It is evident from the table 10 which shows the number of jobs switched for the total sample that there are 195 individuals who made 55.4% of the total sample said that this is their first job, 34% of the sample said that they have switched less than 2 jobs, 26 individuals (7.4%) said that they have switched less than 4 jobs, 5 individuals said that they have switched less than 6 jobs and the only 8 individuals (2%) of the total sample said that they have switched more than 6 jobs.

Time to reach office

Table 11

	Frequency	Percent	Cumulative Percent
Less than 10 minutes	40	11.4	11.4
10-20 minutes	138	39.2	50.6
21-40 minutes	124	35.2	85.8
41-60 minutes	38	10.8	96.6
More than an hour	12	3.4	100.0
Total	352	100.0	

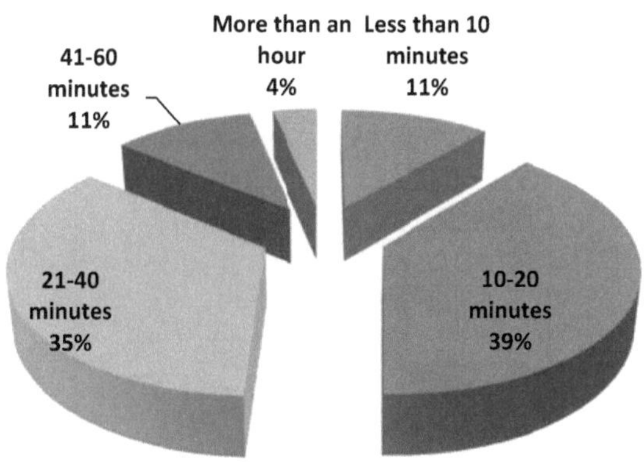

In the time taken to reach office, there are 11.4 respondents said that they reached their offices in less than 10 minutes, 138 individuals consist of 39% of the total sample said that they reached at their offices in 10-20 minutes, 35% of the individuals said that they reached in 21-40 minutes, 38 individuals (10.8%) said that they reached in 41-60 minutes and just 4% respondents said that they reached in their offices in more than an hour.

Nature of Family

Table 12

	Frequency	Percent	Cumulative Percent
Joint family	257	73.0	73.0
Nuclear family	95	27.0	100.0
Total	352	100.0	

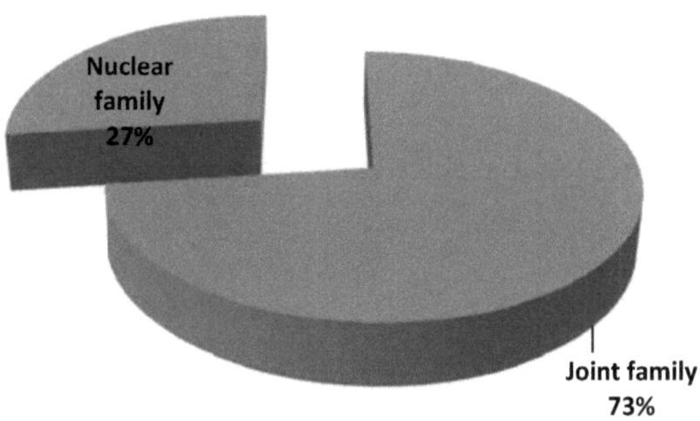

In the nature of family, 257 individuals comprising of 73% of the total sample are joint families and 95 individuals who are 27% of the total sample are nuclear families.

So the highest percentage is of the individuals who have joint families.

Type of House

Table 13

	Frequency	Percent	Cumulative Percent
Your own house	243	69.0	69.0
Rented house	95	27.0	96.0
Leased house	14	4.0	100.0
Total	352	100.0	

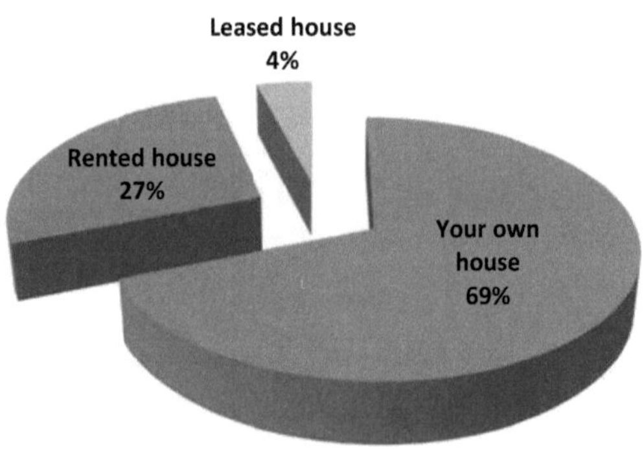

In the type of house, there are 243 individuals who are 69% of the total population have their own houses, 95 individuals (27%) are living in rented houses and just 4% have leased houses.

Type of Conveyance

Table 14

	Frequency	Percent	Cumulative Percent
Personal (car or bike)	270	76.7	76.7
Official	17	4.8	81.5
Auto	21	6.0	87.5
Bus	39	11.1	98.6
Any other	5	1.4	100.0
Total	352	100.0	

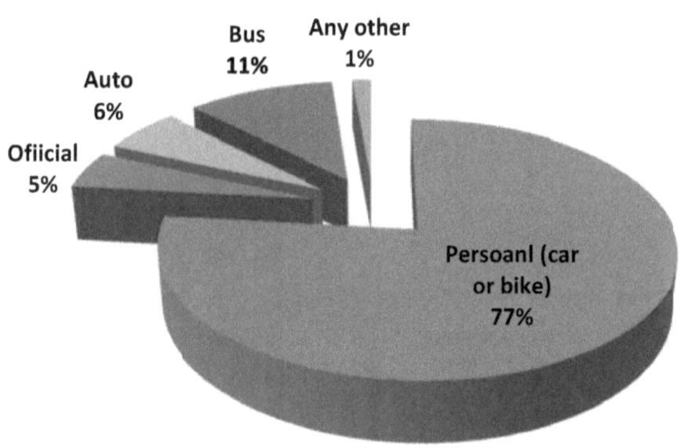

In the type of conveyance that the total sample is using, there are 270 individual who are largest 77% percent of the total population that using their personal conveyance, 17 individuals (4.8%) of the total sample is using official conveyance, 6% is using auto, 11%

is using bus and the rest of just 5 individuals who are 1% of the total sample is using any other type of conveyance.

Number of Dependents

Table 15

	Frequency	Percent	Cumulative Percent
No one	105	29.8	29.8
Less than 3	117	33.2	63.1
3-5	99	28.1	91.2
5-8	30	8.5	99.7
More than 8	1	.3	100.0
Total	352	100.0	

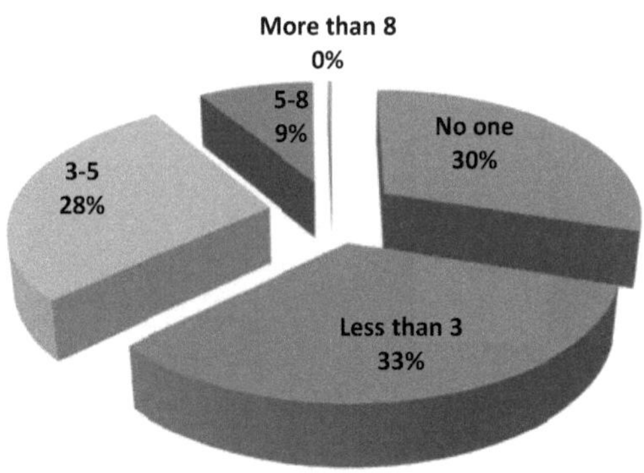

In the number of dependents, there are 105 individual who are 29.8% percent of the total population that have no dependents, 117 individuals (33.2%) of the total sample have less than 3 dependents, 28% have 3-5 dependents, 9% have 5-8 dependents and the just 1individual have more than 8 dependents of the total sample.

Designation

Table 16

	Frequency	Percent	Cumulative Percent
AVP	70	19.9	19.9
OG-I	97	27.6	47.4
OG-II	95	27.0	74.4
OG-III	90	25.6	100.0
Total	352	100.0	

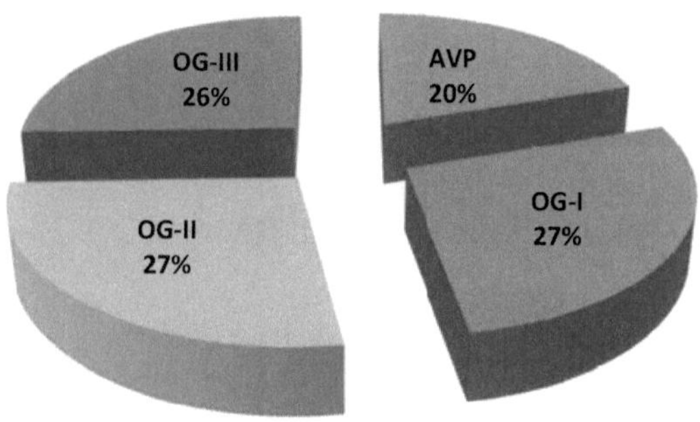

In the designation, 20% of the respondents are the AVP's, 27.6% respondents are officer grade 1, 27% respondents are officer grade 2 and 25.6% respondents are officer grade 3.

Educational Level

Table 17

	Frequency	Percent	Cumulative Percent
High school diploma	8	2.3	2.3
Bachelors degree	165	46.9	49.1
Master's degree	175	49.7	98.9
Doctorate	4	1.1	100.0
Total	352	100.0	

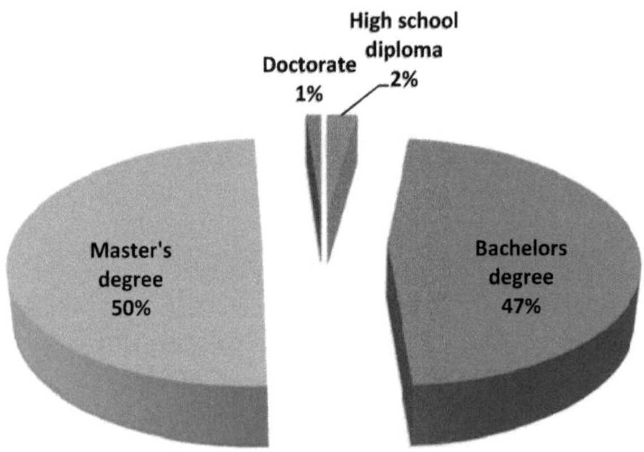

In the research, there are just 8 individuals who are 2.3% of the total sample who have high school diplomas, 165 individuals (47%) have bachelors degree, 175 individuals

(50%) of the total sample have masters degree and the only 1% of the total sample have doctorate degree.

Marital Status

Table 18

	Frequency	Percent	Cumulative Percent
Single	126	35.8	35.8
Married	211	59.9	95.7
Separated	7	2.0	97.7
Divorced	7	2.0	99.7
Widowed	1	.3	100.0
Total	352	100.0	

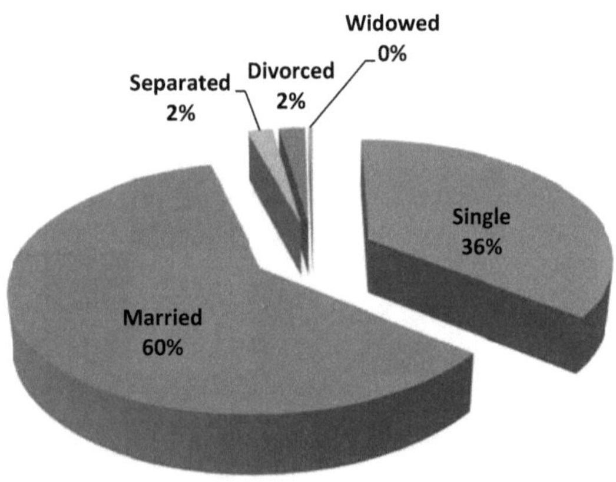

In the research, there are 126 individuals comprising of 35.8% of the total population are single, 60% are married and 2% respondents are separated and divorced.

Comfortable using computers

Table 19

	Frequency	Percent	Cumulative Percent
Very comfortable	176	50.0	50.0
Somewhat comfortable	92	26.1	76.1
Neither comfortable nor uncomfortable	45	12.8	88.9
Somewhat uncomfortable	28	8.0	96.9
Very Uncomfortable	11	3.1	100.0
Total	352	100.0	

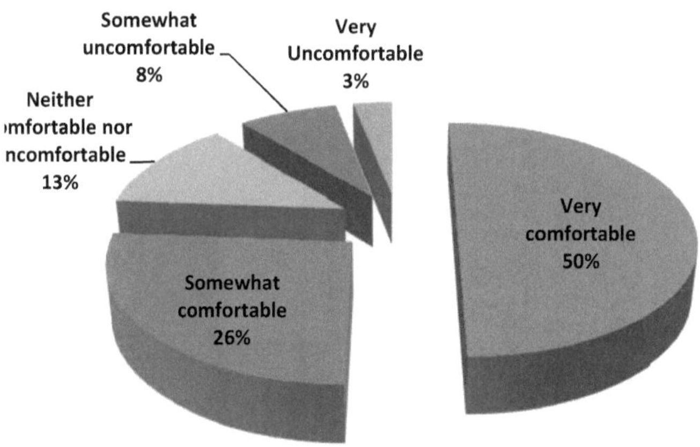

In the research, there are 176 individuals (50%) who said that they are very comfortable in using the computers, 26% of the respondents said that they are somewhat comfortable, 13% of the total sample are neutral and said that they feel neither comfortable nor uncomfortable in using the computers, 8% said that they feel somewhat uncomfortable and only 3% of the total sample said that they are very uncomfortable in using the computers.

Satisfied with internet skills

Table 20

	Frequency	Percent	Cumulative Percent
Very satisfied	160	45.5	45.5
somewhat satisfied	112	31.8	77.3
Neither satisfied nor unsatisfied	46	13.1	90.3
Somewhat unsatisfied	21	6.0	96.3
Very unsatisfied	13	3.7	100.0
Total	352	100.0	

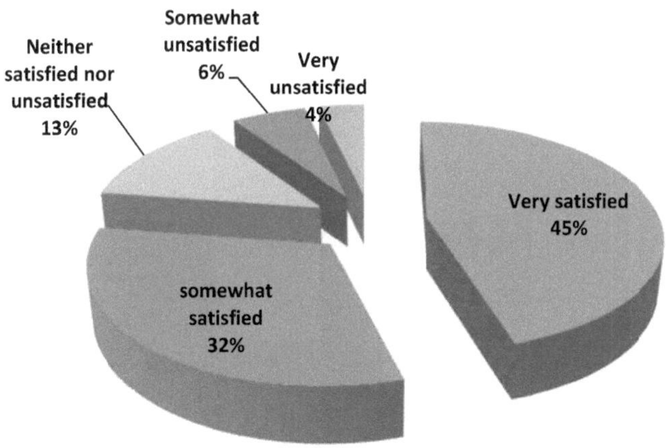

In the research, there are 45% respondents who said that they are very satisfied with their internet skills, 32% of the respondents said that they are somewhat satisfied, 13% of the total sample are neutral and said that they feel neither satisfied nor unsatisfied with their internet skills, 6% said that they feel somewhat unsatisfied and only 4% of the total sample said that they are very unsatisfied with their skills related to internet.

Job Stress: Frequency and Percentages

Huge deal of attention

Table 21

	Frequency	**Percent**	**Cumulative Percent**
Strongly Disagree	7	2.0	2.0
Disagree	32	9.1	11.1
Neutral	46	13.1	24.1
Agree	203	57.7	81.8
Strongly Agree	64	18.2	100.0
Total	352	100.0	

Table 21 shows that 64% of the sample strongly agreed that their work require huge deal of attention, while only 2% contradict it and 13.1% of the respondents are neutral.

Remember different things

Table 22

	Fre-quency	**Percent**	**Cumulative Percent**
Strongly Disag-ree	9	2.6	2.6
Disagree	43	12.2	14.8
Neutral	50	14.2	29.0
Agree	166	47.2	76.1
Strongly Agree	84	23.9	100.0
Total	352	100.0	

There are 23.9% of the sample strongly agreed that in their work they have to remember many different things causing job stress on them, while only 2.6% strongly disagree with it and 14.2% of the respondents are neutral.

Excessive Workload

Table 23

	Frequency	**Percent**	**Cumulative Percent**
Strongly Disagree	11	3.1	3.1
Disagree	70	19.9	23.0
Neutral	82	23.3	46.3
Agree	136	38.6	84.9
Strongly Agree	53	15.1	100.0
Total	352	100.0	

There are 15.1% of the sample strongly agreed and 38.6% sample agreed that they have excessive workload than normal work, while only 3.1% strongly disagree with it and 23.3% of the respondents are neutral.

Could not finish work

Table 24

	Fre-quency	**Percent**	**Cumulative Percent**
Strongly Disagree	20	5.7	5.7
Disagree	113	32.1	37.8
Neutral	67	19.0	56.8
Agree	99	28.1	84.9
Strongly Agree	53	15.1	100.0
Total	352	100.0	

Table 24 shows that 28.1% of the sample agreed that they could not finish their work in a normal work day, while only 5.7% contradict it and 19% of the respondents are neutral.

Forced to work more

Table 25

	Fre-quency	**Percent**	**Cumulative Percent**
Strongly Disagree	35	9.9	9.9
Disagree	88	25.0	34.9
Neutral	82	23.3	58.2
Agree	110	31.3	89.5
Strongly Agree	36	10.2	99.7
Total	352	100.0	

Table 25 shows that 31.3% of the sample agreed that they are forced to work more, while only 9.9% strongly contradict it and 23.3% of the respondents are neutral.

Poor Communication

Table 26

	Fre-quency	**Percent**	**Cumulative Percent**
Strongly Disagree	62	17.6	17.6
Disagree	100	28.4	46.0
Neutral	68	19.3	65.3
Agree	94	26.7	92.0
Strongly Agree	28	8.0	100.0
Total	352	100.0	

26.7% of the sample agreed that there was poor communication in heir office, while 17.6% strongly contradict the statement that there was poor communication in their office.

Unclear responsibilities and roles

Table 27

	Frequency	**Percent**	**Cumulative Percent**
Strongly Disagree	78	22.2	22.2
Disagree	128	36.4	58.5
Neutral	66	18.8	77.3
Agree	60	17.0	94.3
Strongly Agree	20	5.7	100.0
Total	352	100.0	

17% of the sample agreed that their roles and responsibilities in the organization are not clear, while 22.2% strongly contradict it and 18.8% of the respondents are neutral about it.

Conflicts in staff members

Table 28

	Fre-quency	**Percent**	**Cumulative Percent**
Strongly Disagree	67	19.0	19.0
Disagree	106	30.1	49.1
Neutral	68	19.3	68.5
Agree	87	24.7	93.2
Strongly Agree	24	6.8	100.0
Total	352	100.0	

24.7% of the sample agreed that there are conflicts between their staff members, while 19% strongly contradict it and 19.3% of the respondents are neutral about it.

Not receive any appreciation

Table 29

	Frequency	**Percent**	**Cumulative Percent**
Strongly Disagree	38	10.8	10.8
Disagree	111	31.5	42.3
Neutral	74	21.0	63.4
Agree	100	28.4	91.8
Strongly Agree	29	8.2	100.0
Total	352	100.0	

28.4% of the sample agreed that they receive no appreciation from their supervisor or management when their work is really good, while 10.8% strongly contradict it and 21% of the respondents are neutral about it.

Unfair performance evaluation system

Table 30

	Fre-quency	**Percent**	**Cumulative Percent**
Strongly Disagree	34	9.7	9.7
Disagree	118	33.5	43.2
Neutral	80	22.7	65.9
Agree	88	25.0	90.9
Strongly Agree	32	9.1	100.0
Total	352	100.0	

25% of the sample agreed that is unfair performance evaluation system in their organization, while 9.7% strongly contradict it and 22.7% of the respondents are neutral about it.

No opportunities for advancement

Table 31

	Frequency	**Percent**	**Cumulative Percent**
Strongly disagree	44	12.5	12.5
Disagree	128	36.4	48.9
Neutral	77	21.9	70.7
Agree	84	23.9	94.6
Strongly Agree	19	5.4	100.0
Total	352	100.0	

23.9% of the sample agreed that there are no opportunities for advancement in their organization, while 12.5% strongly contradict it and 21.9% of the respondents are neutral about it.

Technological problems

Table 32

	Frequency	**Percent**	**Cumulative Percent**
Strongly Disagree	73	20.7	20.8
Disagree	135	38.4	59.3
Neutral	58	16.5	75.8
Agree	72	20.5	96.3
Strongly Agree	13	3.7	100.0
Total	351	99.7	

20.5% of the sample agreed that they face technological problems in doing their work, while 20.7% strongly contradict it and 16.5% of the respondents are neutral about it.

Age problems

Table 33

	Frequency	**Percent**	**Cumulative Percent**
Strongly Disagree	81	23.0	23.0
Disagree	149	42.3	65.3
Neutral	45	12.8	78.1
Agree	62	17.6	95.7
Strongly Agree	15	4.3	100.0
Total	352	100.0	

17.6% of the sample agreed that there are facing problems due to their age, while 23% strongly contradict it and 12.8% of the respondents are neutral about it.

Level of noise in working area

Table 34

	Frequency	**Percent**	**Cumulative Percent**
Strongly Disagree	36	10.2	10.2
Disagree	127	36.1	46.3
Neutral	73	20.7	67.0
Agree	91	25.9	92.9
Strongly Agree	25	7.1	100.0
Total	352	100.0	

25.9% of the sample agreed that their working area is very noisy, while 10.2% strongly contradict it and 20.7% of the respondents are neutral about it.

Extremely crowded area

Table 35

	Frequency	**Percent**	**Cumulative Percent**
Strongly Disagree	33	9.4	9.4
Disagree	122	34.7	44.0
Neutral	74	21.0	65.1
Agree	103	29.3	94.3
Strongly Agree	20	5.7	100.0
Total	352	100.0	

29.3% of the sample agreed that their working area is extremely crowded, while 9.4% strongly contradict it and 21% of the respondents are neutral about it.

Boss Pressure

Table 36

	Frequency	**Percent**	**Cumulative Percent**
Strongly Disagree	45	12.8	12.8
Disagree	150	42.6	55.4
Neutral	70	19.9	75.3
Agree	73	20.7	96.0
Strongly Agree	14	4.0	100.0
Total	352	100.0	

20.7% of the sample agreed that they face the boss pressure to work more, while 12.8% strongly contradict it and 19.9% of the respondents are neutral about it.

No emotional attachment

Table 37

	Frequency	**Percent**	**Cumulative Percent**
Strongly Disagree	47	13.4	13.4
Disagree	125	35.5	48.9
Neutral	71	20.2	69.0
Agree	90	25.6	94.6
Strongly Agree	19	5.4	100.0
Total	352	100.0	

25.6% of the sample agreed that they feel no emotional attachment with their organization, while 13.4% strongly contradict it and 20.2% of the respondents are neutral about it.

Boss shouting

Table 38

	Fre-quency	**Percent**	**Cumulative Percent**
Strongly Disagree	89	25.3	25.3
Disagree	144	40.9	66.2
Neutral	57	16.2	82.4
Agree	51	14.5	96.9
Strongly Agree	11	3.1	100.0
Total	352	100.0	

14.5% of the sample agreed that their boss shouts at them, while 25.3% strongly contradict it and 16.2% of the respondents are neutral about it.

Leg pullying behavior

Table 39

	Fre-quency	**Percent**	**Cumulative Percent**
Strongly Disag-ree	54	15.3	15.3
Disagree	126	35.8	51.1
Neutral	90	25.6	76.7
Agree	68	19.3	96.0
Strongly Agree	14	4.0	100.0
Total	352	100.0	

19.3% of the sample agreed that they face leg pulling behavior from their colleagues, while 15.3% strongly contradict it and 25.6% of the respondents are neutral about it.

Uncomfortable workplace

Table 40

	Frequency	**Percent**	**Cumulative Percent**
Strongly Disagree	72	20.5	20.5
Disagree	144	40.9	61.4
Neutral	64	18.2	79.5
Agree	54	15.3	94.9
Strongly Agree	18	5.1	100.0
Total	352	100.0	

15.3% of the sample agreed that their workplace is very uncomfortable, while 20.5% strongly contradict it and 18.2% of the respondents are neutral about it.

Unsatisfied with salary and rewards

Table 41

	Fre-quency	**Percent**	**Cumulative Percent**
Strongly Disag-ree	46	13.1	13.1
Disagree	109	31.0	44.0
Neutral	66	18.8	62.8
Agree	92	26.1	88.9
Strongly Agree	39	11.1	100.0
Total	352	100.0	

26.1% of the sample agreed that they are unsatisfied with their salary rewards, while 13.1% strongly contradict it and 18.8% of the respondents are neutral about it.

Long working hours

Table 42

	Frequency	**Percent**	**Cumulative Percent**
Strongly Disagree	46	13.1	13.1
Disagree	120	34.1	47.2
Neutral	83	23.6	70.7
Agree	79	22.4	93.2
Strongly Agree	24	6.8	100.0
Total	352	100.0	

22.4% of the sample agreed that there are very long working hours in their organization, while 13.1% strongly contradict it and 23.6% of the respondents are neutral about it.

CWB: Frequency and Percentages

Purposely damaged equipment/property

Table 43

	Fre-quency	Percent	Cumulative Percent
Never	126	35.8	35.8
Rarely	114	32.4	68.2
Sometimes	59	16.8	84.9
Quite Of-ten	36	10.2	95.2
Very Often	17	4.8	100.0
Total	352	100.0	

4.8% of the respondents agreed that they purposely destroyed their organization equipments very often, 10.2 agreed that they are doing this quite often, 16.8% said sometimes, 32.4% said rarely while 35.8% said that they never purposely damaged their organizational property.

Purposely wasted materials/supplies

Table 44

	Frequency	**Percent**	**Cumulative Percent**
Never	117	33.2	33.2
Rarely	126	35.8	69.0
Sometimes	60	17.0	86.1
Quite Often	30	8.5	94.6
Very Often	19	5.4	100.0
Total	352	100.0	

5.4% of the respondents agreed that they purposely wasted their organization materials or supplies very often, 8.5 agreed that they are doing this quite often, 17% said sometimes, 35.8% said rarely while 33.2% said that they never purposely wasted their organizational supplies.

Come to work late without permission

Table 45

	Frequency	**Percent**	**Cumulative Percent**
Never	123	34.9	34.9
Rarely	104	29.5	64.5
Sometimes	66	18.8	83.2
Quite Often	33	9.4	92.6
Very Often	26	7.4	100.0
Total	352	100.0	

7.4% of the respondents agreed that they came to work late without permission very often, 9.4 agreed that they are doing this quite often, 18.8% said sometimes, 29.5% said rarely while 34.9% said that they never came to work late.

Stayed home to avoid home

Table 46

	Frequency	**Percent**	**Cumulative Percent**
Never	148	42.0	42.0
Rarely	90	25.6	67.6
Sometimes	64	18.2	85.8
Quite Often	24	6.8	92.6
Very Often	26	7.4	100.0
Total	352	100.0	

7.4% of the respondents agreed that they stayed at home to avoid work very often, 6.8% agreed that they are doing this quite often, 18.2% said sometimes, 25.6% said rarely while 42% said that they never stayed at home to avoid work.

Taken a longer break

Table 47

	Frequency	**Percent**	**Cumulative Percent**
Never	145	41.2	41.2
Rarely	79	22.4	63.6
Sometimes	81	23.0	86.6
Quite Often	29	8.2	94.9
Very Often	18	5.1	100.0
Total	352	100.0	

4.8% of the respondents agreed that they take a longer break than they were allowed to take very often, 8.2 agreed that they are doing this quite often, 23% said sometimes, 22.4% said rarely while 41.2% said that they never taken a longer break than normal.

Left work earlier than allowed

Table 48

	Frequency	**Percent**	**Cumulative Percent**
Never	165	46.9	46.9
Rarely	77	21.9	68.8
Sometimes	73	20.7	89.5
Quite Often	18	5.1	94.6
Very Often	19	5.4	100.0
Total	352	100.0	

5.4% of the respondents agreed that they left work earlier than were allowed very often, 5.1 agreed that they are doing this quite often, 20.7% said sometimes, 21.9% said rarely while 46.9% said that they never left work earlier.

Purposely work incorrectly

Table 49

	Frequency	**Percent**	**Cumulative Percent**
Never	203	57.7	57.7
Rarely	62	17.6	75.3
Sometimes	54	15.3	90.6
Quite Often	16	4.5	95.2
Very Often	17	4.8	100.0
Total	352	100.0	

4.8% of the respondents agreed that they purposely did the work incorrectly very often, 4.5 agreed that they are doing this quite often, 15.3% said sometimes, 17.6% said rarely while 57.7% said that they never purposely did incorrect work.

Purposely don't follow instructions

Table 50

	Frequency	**Percent**	**Cumulative Percent**
Never	201	57.1	57.1
Rarely	81	23.0	80.1
Sometimes	49	13.9	94.0
Quite Often	13	3.7	97.7
Very Often	8	2.3	100.0
Total	352	100.0	

Only 2.3% of the respondents agreed that they purposely don't follow the instructions very often, 3.7 agreed that they are doing this quite often, 13.9% said sometimes, 23% said rarely while 57.1% said that they never did it.

Stole something of colleagues

Table 51

	Fre-quency	Percent	Cumulative Percent
Never	240	68.2	68.2
Rarely	56	15.9	84.1
Sometimes	39	11.1	95.2
Quite Often	14	4.0	99.1
Very Often	3	.9	100.0
Total	352	100.0	

Only 1% of the respondents agreed that they stole something belonging to their colleagues at work very often, 4% agreed that they are doing this quite often, 11.1% said sometimes, 15.9% said rarely while 68.2% said that they never did it.

Took supplies home

Table 52

	Frequency	**Percent**	**Cumulative Percent**
Never	234	66.5	66.5
Rarely	51	14.5	81.0
Sometimes	51	14.5	95.5
Quite Often	12	3.4	98.9
Very Often	4	1.1	100.0
Total	352	100.0	

Only 1.1% of the respondents agreed that they purposely took their organizational supplies to home without permission very often, 3.4% agreed that they are doing this quite often, 14.5% said sometimes, 14.5% said rarely while 66.5% said that they never did it.

Took money of your employer

Table 53

	Frequency	**Percent**	**Cumulative Percent**
Never	263	74.7	74.7
Rarely	44	12.5	87.2
Sometimes	32	9.1	96.3
Quite Often	9	2.6	98.9
Very Often	4	1.1	100.0
Total	352	100.0	

Only 1.1% of the respondents agreed that they took the money from their employer without permission very often, 2.6 agreed that they are doing this quite often, 9.1% said sometimes, 12.5% said rarely while 74.7% said that they never did it.

Stole something of someone

Table 54

	Frequency	**Percent**	**Cumulative Percent**
Never	262	74.4	74.4
Rarely	50	14.2	88.6
Sometimes	29	8.2	96.9
Quite Often	8	2.3	99.1
Very Often	3	.9	100.0
Total	352	100.0	

Only 1% of the respondents agreed that they stole something belonging to someone at work very often, 2.3% agreed that they are doing this quite often, 8.2% said sometimes, 14.2% said rarely while 74.4% said that they never did it.

Been nasty or rude to customers

Table 55

	Frequency	**Percent**	**Cumulative Percent**
Never	242	68.8	68.8
Rarely	61	17.3	86.1
Sometimes	33	9.4	95.5
Quite Often	11	3.1	98.6
Very Often	5	1.4	100.0
Total	352	100.0	

Only 1.4% of the respondents agreed that they been nasty or rude to customers very often, 3.1% agreed that they are doing this quite often, 9.4% said sometimes, 17.3% said rarely while 68.8% said that they never did it.

Insulted someone

Table 56

	Fre-quency	**Percent**	**Cumulative Percent**
Never	242	68.8	68.8
Rarely	58	16.5	85.2
Sometimes	32	9.1	94.3
Quite Often	17	4.8	99.1
Very Often	3	.9	100.0
Total	352	100.0	

Only 1% of the respondents agreed that they insulted someone about their job performance very often, 4.8% agreed that they are doing this quite often, 9.1% said sometimes, 16.5% said rarely while 68.8% said that they never did it.

Ignored someone at work

Table 57

	Fre-quency	**Percent**	**Cumulative Percent**
Never	230	65.3	65.3
Rarely	65	18.5	83.8
Sometimes	43	12.2	96.0
Quite Of-ten	12	3.4	99.4
Very Often	2	.6	100.0
Total	352	100.0	

Only 0.6% of the respondents agreed that they stole ignored someone at work very often, 3.4% agreed that they are doing this quite often, 12.2% said sometimes, 18.5% said rarely while 65.3% said that they never did it.

Blamed someone for error you made

Table 58

	Frequency	**Percent**	**Cumulative Percent**
Never	246	69.9	69.9
Rarely	56	15.9	85.8
Sometimes	30	8.5	94.3
Quite Often	16	4.5	98.9
Very Often	4	1.1	100.0
Total	352	100.0	

Only 1.1% of the respondents agreed that they blamed someone at work for the error they made very often, 4.5% agreed that they are doing this quite often, 8.5% said sometimes, 15.9% said rarely while 69.9% said that they never did it.

Started an argument

Table 59

	Fre-quency	**Percent**	**Cumulative Percent**
Never	225	63.9	63.9
Rarely	66	18.8	82.7
Sometimes	41	11.6	94.3
Quite Often	16	4.5	98.9
Very Often	4	1.1	100.0
Total	352	100.0	

Only 1.1% of the respondents agreed that they started an argument with someone at work very often, 4.5% agreed that they are doing this quite often, 11.6% said sometimes, 18.8% said rarely while 63.9% said that they never did it.

Verbally abused someone

Table 60

	Frequency	**Percent**	**Cumulative Percent**
Never	268	76.1	76.1
Rarely	50	14.2	90.3
Sometimes	23	6.5	96.9
Quite Often	8	2.3	99.1
Very Often	3	.9	100.0
Total	352	100.0	

Only 1% of the respondents agreed that they verbally abused someone at work very often, 2.3% agreed that they are doing this quite often, 6.5% said sometimes, 14.2% said rarely while 76.1% said that they never did it.

Threatened someone

Table 61

	Fre-quency	**Percent**	**Cumulative Percent**
Never	274	77.8	77.8
Rarely	51	14.5	92.3
Sometimes	21	6.0	98.3
Quite often	6	1.7	100.0
Total	352	100.0	

Only 1.7% of the respondents agreed that they threatened someone at work quite often, 6% said sometimes, 14.5% said rarely while 77.8% said that they never did it.

Said something to others

Table 62

	Fre-quency	Percent	Cumulative Percent
Never	257	73.0	73.0
Rarely	56	15.9	88.9
Sometimes	26	7.4	96.3
Quite Often	9	2.6	98.9
Very Often	4	1.1	100.0
Total	352	100.0	

Only 1.1% of the respondents agreed that they said something to someone at work to make them feel bad very often, 2.6% agreed that they are doing this quite often, 7.4% said sometimes, 15.9% said rarely while 73% said that they never did it.

Looked at someone's private mails

Table 63

	Frequency	**Percent**	**Cumulative Percent**
Never	273	77.6	77.6
Rarely	44	12.5	90.1
Sometimes	25	7.1	97.2
Quite Often	8	2.3	99.4
Very Often	2	.6	100.0
Total	352	100.0	

Only 0.6% of the respondents agreed that they looked at someone private mails without permission very often, 2.3% agreed that they are doing this quite often, 7.1% said sometimes, 12.5% said rarely while 77.6% said that they never did it.

Insulted or made fun of someone

Table 64

	Frequency	**Percent**
Never	259	73.6
Rarely	50	14.2
Sometimes	34	9.7
Quite Often	6	1.7
Very Often	3	.9
Total	352	100.0

Only 1% of the respondents agreed that they stole insulted or made fun of someone at work very often, 1.7% agreed that they are doing this quite often, 9.7% said sometimes, 14.2% said rarely while 73.6% said that they never did it.

Cross Tab Analysis

Age * Doing this job for * Gender Cross tabulation

Table 65

Gender			Doing this job for					Total
			Few months less than 1 year	1-3 years	3-6 years	6-9 years	More than 9 years	
Male	Age	Under 26	16	23	3	1	0	43
		26-35	4	28	32	20	6	90
		36-45	0	5	22	24	30	81
		46-55	0	2	3	1	38	44
		56+	0	1	0	1	16	18
	Total		**20**	**59**	**60**	**47**	**90**	**276**
Female	Age	Under 26	12	9	2	0	1	24
		26-35	1	12	21	2	0	36
		36-45	0	0	2	4	5	11
		46-55	0	0	0	0	2	2
		56+	0	0	0	0	3	3
	Total		**13**	**21**	**25**	**6**	**11**	**76**

The table show the multiple view doing this job, age and gender wise, the table shows that 16 males who are under 26 years of age doing their jobs for less than a year, 23 male doing it from 1-3 years, 3 males doing it from 3-6 years and no one does this for more than 9 years. In age group of 26-35 years, 28 males doing their jobs for 1-3 years, 32 doing for 3-6 years, 20 doing this for 6-9 years and only 6 doing their jobs for more than 9 years. In 36-45 years age bracket, 22 males doing their jobs for 3-6 years, 24 for 6-9 years and 30 for more than 9 years. In the same way males 16 who are 56+ of age doing their jobs for more than 9 years.

Likewise the table shows that 12 females who are under 26 years of age doing their jobs for less than a year, 9 doing it from 1-3 years, 2 doing it from 3-6 years and only one female does this for more than 9 years. In age group of 26-35 years, 12 females were doing their jobs for 1-3 years, 21 doing for 3-6 years, 2 doing this for 6-9 years and no one doing their jobs for more than 9 years. In 36-45 years age bracket, 2 females doing their jobs for 3-6 years, 4 for 6-9 years and 5 for more than 9 years. In the same way 3 females who are 56+ of age doing their jobs for more than 9 years.

Total professional experience * Jobs switched * Gender Cross tabulation

Table 66

Gender			Jobs switched: No its my first job	Less than 2	Less than 4	Less than 6	More than 6	Total
Male	Total professional experience	Few months less than 1 year	11	2	1	0	0	14
		1-3 years	32	20	1	0	0	53
		3-6 years	25	21	4	0	1	51
		6-9 years	16	19	5	0	0	40
		More than 9 years	58	36	13	5	6	118
	Total		**142**	**98**	**24**	**5**	**7**	**276**
Female	Total professional experience	Few months less than 1 year	11	0	0	0	0	11
		1-3 years	14	7	0	0	0	21
		3-6 years	18	5	1	0	0	24
		6-9 years	3	3	0	0	0	6
		More than 9 years	7	5	1	0	1	14
	Total		**53**	**20**	**2**	**0**	**1**	**76**

The table shows the multiple view from jobs switched, total professional experience and gender wise, the results shoes that there are 11 males who have total professional experience for less than a year have said that it is their first job, 2 have switched less than 2 jobs and only 1 have switched less than 4 jobs. 32 males who have experience for 1-3 years said that it is their first job, 20 males have switched less than 2 jobs, and only 1 has switch less than 4 jobs. 25 males of professional experience for 3-6 years said that it is their first job and 21 have switched less than 2 jobs. Similarly 58 individuals having total professional experience of more than 9 years said that this is their first job, 36 have switched less than 2 jobs, 13 have switched less than 4 jobs, 5 individuals have switched less than 6 jobs and 6 males have switched more than 6 jobs. This table also shows that the males having professional experience of more than 9 years have switched their jobs most and facing more job stress than others.

Similarly 11 females who have total professional experience for less than a year have said that it is their first job and no have switched any jobs. 14 females who have experience for 1-3 years said that it is their first job and 7 females have switched less than 2 jobs. 18 females of professional experience for 3-6 years said that it is their first job and 5 have switched less than 2 jobs. Similarly 7 individuals having total professional experience of more than 9 years said that this is their first job, 5 have switched less than 2 jobs, 1 have switched less than 4 jobs and only 1 female have switch more than 6 jobs.

Designation in bank * Educational level attained * Gender Cross tabulation

Table 67

Gender			Educational level attained				Total
			High school diploma	Bachelors degree	Master's degree	Doctora-te	
Male	Designation in bank	AVP	3	28	28	0	59
		OG-I	1	39	37	1	78
		OG-II	1	36	30	1	68
		OG-III	0	32	38	1	71
	Total		**5**	**135**	**133**	**3**	**276**
Female	Designation in bank	AVP	2	4	5	0	11
		OG-I	1	5	13	0	19
		OG-II	0	15	11	1	27
		OG-III	0	6	13	0	19
	Total		**3**	**30**	**42**	**1**	**76**

The table shows the multiple views from designation, education level attained and gender wise, the table shows that there are 3 male AVP's who have high school diplomas, 28 AVP's have bachelor and masters degree and no one have doctorate degree. 1male officer of grade-I have high school diploma 39 have bachelor degree and 37 have masters degree. 1 male officer of grade-II have high school diploma36 have bachelors degree and 30 have masters degree. Similarly 32 males officer of grade-III have bachelor degree, 38 males have masters degree and only I male OG-III have doctorate degree. These results show that the most of the sample have bachelors and masters degree. Similarly, there are 2 female AVP's who have high school diplomas, 4 AVP's have bachelor, 5 have master's degree and no one have doctorate degree. 1female officer of grade-I have high school diploma 5 have bachelor degree and 11 have masters degree. No female officer of grade-II have high school diploma, 15 have bachelor's degree and 11 have master's degree. Similarly 6 females officer of grade-III have bachelor degree and13 females have masters degree.

Designation in bank * Comfortable using computers * Gender Cross tabulation

Table 68

Gender			**Comfortable using computers**					**Total**
			Very comfortable	**Somewhat comfortable**	**Neither comfortable nor uncomfortable**	**Somewhat uncomfortable**	**Very Uncomfortable**	
Male	Designation in bank	AVP	15	27	9	5	3	59
		OG-I	30	24	16	6	2	78
		OG-II	44	11	7	5	1	68
		OG-III	45	17	4	2	3	71
	Total		**134**	**79**	**36**	**18**	**9**	**276**
Female	Designation in bank	AVP	2	5	1	2	1	11
		OG-I	8	3	4	4	0	19
		OG-II	19	4	1	2	1	27
		OG-III	13	1	3	2	0	19
	Total		**42**	**13**	**9**	**10**	**2**	**76**

The table shows the multiple views from designation, comfortable using computers and gender wise, the table shows that there are 15 male AVP's who feel very comfortable in using the computers, 27 male AVP's feel somewhat comfortable, 9 AVP's feel neither comfortable nor uncomfortable , 5 feel somewhat uncomfortable and only 3 are feeling very uncomfortable. 30 male officer of grade-I are very comfortable in using the computers, 24 feel somewhat comfortable, 16 feel neither comfortable nor uncomfortable , 6 feel somewhat uncomfortable and only 2 are feeling very uncomfortable. 44 male officers of grade-II are very comfortable in using the computers, 11 feel somewhat comfortable, 7 feel neither comfortable nor uncomfortable, 5 feel somewhat uncomfortable and only 1 are feeling very uncomfortable. In the same way 45 officers of grade-III are very comfortable in using the computers, 17 feel somewhat comfortable, 4 feel neither comfortable nor uncomfortable, 2 feel somewhat uncomfortable nor only 3 are feeling very uncomfortable. The results show that majority of the males respondents feel comfortable using the computers.

Similarly, there are 2 female AVP's who feel very comfortable in using the computers, 5 female AVP's feel somewhat comfortable, 1 AVP's feel neither comfortable nor uncomfortable , 2 feel somewhat uncomfortable and only 1 are feeling very uncomfortable. 8 female officer of grade-I are very comfortable in using the computers, 3 feel somewhat comfortable, 4 feel neither comfortable nor uncomfortable , 4 feel somewhat uncomfortable and no one are feeling very uncomfortable. 19 female officers of grade-II are very comfortable in using the computers, 4 feel somewhat comfortable, 1 feel neither comfortable nor uncomfortable, 2 feel somewhat uncomfortable and only 1 are feeling very uncomfortable. In the same way 13 female officers of grade-III are very comfortable in using the computers, 1 feel somewhat comfortable, 3 feel neither comfortable nor uncomfortable, 2 feel somewhat uncomfortable no one are feeling very uncomfortable.

Advanced Statistical Tests

H0: The job stress and CWB level among sample is same.
H1: Job stress and CWB level is not same.

Two Independent sample test

Gender and nature of family is not normally distributed across the sample so we will apply two independent sample test as it has only two classes.

Table 69

No.	Test Variables	Grouping Variables	Mean Ranks		Z- value	P-value
			Male	Female		
1	job stress	Gender	176.25	177.40	-0.087	0.931
	CWB		182.03	156.40	-1.946	0.052
			Joint	Nuclear		
2	job Stress	Nature of Family	186	150.79	-2.882	0.004
	CWB		180.41	165.91	-1.188	0.235

1. In gender, the p-value for job stress is 0.931 > 0.05 so we accept Ho which says that male and females have same job stress level. Similarly for CWB, the p-value is 0.052 > 0.05 so we again accept Ho which says that CWB is same among males and females.

2. In nature of family, the p-value for job stress is 0.004 < 0.05 so we reject Ho and accept H1which says that job stress level between males and females is not same and by further looking at their means it is evident that joint families have facing more stress. Similarly for CWB, the p-value is 0.235 > 0.05 so we accept Ho which says that CWB is same among joint and nuclear families.

ANOVA

The time to reach office and educational level is normally distributed so we apply parametric test for more than 2 classes which is ANOVA.

Time to Reach Office

Table 70

		Sum of Squares	**df**	**Mean Square**	**F**	**Sig.**
Variable 1: Job Stress	Between Groups	5.434	4	1.358	2.312	.057
	Within Groups	203.915	347	.588		
	Total	209.348	351			
Variable 2: CWB	Between Groups	6.330	4	1.582	3.036	.018
	Within Groups	180.867	347	.521		
	Total	187.197	351			

The sigma value for time to reach office for job stress is 0.057 > 0.05 showed that there is no significant difference in all individuals who are who have different times to reach their office from their house. Similarly in CWB the sigma value is 0.018 < 0.05 showed that CWB was significantly different in all the individuals.

Educational Level

Table 71

		Sum of Squares	df	Mean Square	F	Sig.
Variable 1: Job Stress	Between Groups	.605	3	.202	.336	.799
	Within Groups	208.743	348	.600		
	Total	209.348	351			
Variable 2: CWB	Between Groups	.853	3	.284	.531	.661
	Within Groups	186.344	348	.535		
	Total	187.197	351			

The sigma value for educational level is 0.799 > 0.05 showed that that stress was significantly equal in all individuals who are who have different education. Similarly in CWB the sigma value is 0.661 > 0.05 showed that CWB was significantly equal in all the individuals.

Kruskal-Wallis Test

Age

Table 72

	Age	N	Mean Rank	Sigma Value
Variable 1: Job Stress	Under 26	67	179.43	
	26-35	126	170.10	
	36-45	92	190.40	0.137
	46-55	46	149.58	
	56+	21	203.64	
	Total	352		
Variable 2: CWB	Under 26	67	139.19	
	26-35	126	168.56	
	36-45	92	184.66	0.000
	46-55	46	213.09	
	56+	21	227.29	
	Total	352		

In Kruskal Wallis test for age, the sigma value for job stress is 0.137 > 0.05 showed that stress was significantly equal in all age groups.

Similarly in CWB, the sigma value is $0.000 < 0.05$ showed that counter-productive work behavior was significantly not equal in all age groups and by looking at means it is evident that the individuals who are the age of 56+ are more involved in CWB than other individuals.

Monthly Salary

Table 73

	Monthly Salary	N	Mean Rank	Sigma value
Variable 1: Job Stress	Less than 25,000	76	194.26	
	25,000-40,000	128	172.29	
	40,001-55,000	75	181.75	0.302
	55,001-70,000	41	164.72	
	More than 70,000	32	153.94	
	Total	352		
Variable 2: CWB	Less than 25,000	76	146.86	
	25,000-40,000	128	182.13	
	40,001-55,000	75	175.61	0.032
	55,001-70,000	41	204.52	
	More than 70,000	32	190.56	
	Total	352		

In Kruskal Wallis test for monthly salary, the sigma value for job stress is 0.302 > 0.05 showed that stress was significantly equal in all individuals getting different salaries.

Similarly in CWB, the sigma value is 0.032 < 0.05 showed that counter-productive work behavior was significantly not equal in all individuals earning different salaries and by looking at their mean ranks it is evident that the individuals who are earning the salary of 55,001-70,000 are more involved in CWB.

Doing this job for

Table 74

	Doing this job for	N	Mean Rank	Sigma value
Variable 1: Job Stress	Few months less than 1 year	33	191.35	
	1-3 years	80	190.46	
	3-6 years	85	147.14	0.034
	6-9 years	53	191.15	
	More than 9 years	101	177.62	
	Total	352		
Variable 2: CWB	Few months less than 1 year	33	143.95	
	1-3 years	80	172.30	
	3-6 years	85	160.09	0.011
	6-9 years	53	177.38	
	More than 9 years	101	203.81	
	Total	352		

In Kruskal Wallis test for individuals doing job, the sigma value for job stress is $0.034 < 0.05$ showed that stress was significantly not equal in all individuals.

Similarly in CWB, the sigma value is $0.011 < 0.05$ showed that counter-productive work behavior was also significantly not equal in all individuals doing their current jobs and it is evident from their mean ranks that the individuals who are doing their jobs for more than 9 years are more involved in CWB.

Nature of job

Table 75

	Nature of job	N	Mean Rank	Sigma value
Variable 1: Job Stress	You have to work in this office	242	173.63	
	You have a field job	30	185.53	0.724
	Both office and field job	80	181.79	
	Total	352		
Variable 2: CWB	You have to work in this office	242	162.68	
	You have a field job	30	207.63	0.001
	Both office and field job	80	206.63	
	Total	352		

In Kruskal Wallis test for nature of job, the sigma value for job stress is 0.724 > 0.05 showed that stress was significantly equal in all individuals doing different nature of jobs.

Similarly in CWB, the sigma value is $0.001 < 0.05$ showed that counter-productive work behavior was significantly not equal in all individuals doing different nature of jobs and it is evident that the individuals who have a field job are more involved in CWB.

Total Professional Experience

Table 76

	Total professional experience	**N**	**Mean Rank**	**Sigma value**
Variable 1: Job Stress	Few months less than 1 year	25	205.98	
	1-3 years	74	185.94	
	3-6 years	75	157.39	0.165
	6-9 years	46	190.11	
	More than 9 years	132	171.74	
	Total	352		
Variable 2: CWB	Few months less than 1 year	25	150.14	
	1-3 years	74	163.72	
	3-6 years	75	169.85	0.160
	6-9 years	46	175.38	
	More than 9 years	132	192.83	
	Total	352		

In Kruskal Wallis test for total professional experience, the sigma value for job stress is 0.165 > 0.05 showed that stress was significantly equal in all individuals having different professional experiences.

Similarly in CWB, the sigma value is 0.160 > 0.05 showed that counter-productive work behavior was also significantly equal in all individuals.

Jobs Switched

Table 77

	Jobs switched	N	Mean Rank	Sigma value
Variable 1: Job Stress	No its my first job	195	188.79	
	Less than 2	118	152.00	
	Less than 4	26	181.13	
	Less than 6	5	225.50	0.025
	More than 6	8	192.63	
	Total	352		
Variable 2: CWB	No its my first job	195	181.11	
	Less than 2	118	171.11	
	Less than 4	26	151.81	0.503
	Less than 6	5	205.60	
	More than 6	8	205.69	
	Total	352		

In Kruskal Wallis test for numbers of job switched, the sigma value for job stress is 0.025 < 0.05 showed that there is significant difference in all individuals and the results shows that the individuals who have switched less than 6 jobs are facing more stress than others.

Similarly in CWB, the sigma value is 0.503 > 0.05 showed that there is no significant difference between all individuals switching different jobs.

Type of House

Table 78

	House in which live in	**N**	**Mean Rank**	**Sigma value**
Variable 1: Job Stress	Your own house	243	178.81	
	Rented house	95	175.77	
	Leased house	14	141.39	0.407
	Total	352		
Variable 2: CWB	Your own house	243	172.44	
	Rented house	95	190.44	0.227
	Leased house	14	152.32	
	Total	352		

In Kruskal Wallis test for individuals having different types of house, the sigma value for job stress is 0.407 > 0.05 showed that stress was significantly equal in all individuals living in different houses.

Similarly in CWB, the sigma value is 0.227 > 0.05 showed that counter-productive work behavior was also significantly equal in all individuals.

Type of Conveyance

Table 79

	Type of conveyance	**N**	**Mean Rank**	**Sigma value**
Variable 1: Job Stress	Personal (car or bike)	270	177.77	
	Official	17	155.68	
	Auto	21	144.45	
	Bus	39	195.42	0.374
	Any other	5	165.80	
	Total	352		
Variable 2: CWB	Personal (car or bike)	270	173.85	
	Official	17	212.03	
	Auto	21	152.62	0.373
	Bus	39	191.04	
	Any other	5	185.50	
	Total	352		

In Kruskal Wallis test for individuals using different conveyances, the sigma value for job stress is 0.374 > 0.05 showed that stress was significantly equal in all individuals using different conveyances.

Similarly in CWB, the sigma value is 0.373 > 0.05 showed that counter-productive work behavior was also significantly not equal in all individuals using different conveyances.

No. of dependents

Table 80

	No of dependents	N	Mean Rank	Sigma value
Variable 1: Job Stress	No one	105	178.12	
	Less than 3	117	181.91	
	3-5	99	159.12	
	5-8	30	208.32	0.177
	More than 8	1	140.00	
	Total	352		
Variable 2: CWB	No one	105	164.76	
	Less than 3	117	199.57	
	3-5	99	153.74	
	5-8	30	199.58	0.005
	More than 8	1	271.00	
	Total	352		

In Kruskal Wallis test for number of dependents, the sigma value for job stress is 0.177 > 0.05 showed that stress was significantly equal in all individuals having different number of dependents.

Similarly in CWB, the sigma value is 0.005 < 0.05 showed that counter-productive work behavior was significantly not equal in all individuals having different dependents.

Designation

Table 81

	Designation in bank	N	Mean Rank	Sigma value
Variable 1: Job Stress	AVP	70	171.91	
	OG-I	97	170.43	
	OG-II	95	163.95	0.083
	OG-III	90	199.86	
	Total	352		
Variable 2: CWB	AVP	70	176.47	
	OG-I	97	193.72	
	OG-II	95	168.88	0.234
	OG-III	90	166.01	
	Total	352		

In Kruskal Wallis test for individuals who are at different designations, the sigma value for job stress is 0.083 > 0.05 showed that stress was significantly equal in all individuals at different designations.

Similarly in CWB, the sigma value is 0.234 > 0.05 showed that counter-productive work behavior was significantly equal in all individuals.

Comfortable using computers

Table 82

	Comfortable using computers	N	Mean Rank	Sigma value
Variable 1: Job Stress	Very comfortable	176	161.28	
	Somewhat comfortable	92	187.13	
	Neither comfortable nor uncomfortable	45	227.78	0.000
	Somewhat uncomfortable	28	143.25	
	Very Uncomfortable	11	205.95	
	Total	352		
Variable 2: CWB	Very comfortable	176	143.54	
	Somewhat comfortable	92	207.32	
	Neither comfortable nor uncomfortable	45	202.69	0.000
	Somewhat uncomfortable	28	225.75	
	Very Uncomfortable	11	213.68	
	Total	352		

In Kruskal Wallis test for individuals using computers, the sigma value for job stress is 0.000 < 0.05 showed that stress was significantly not equal in all individuals and the stress is faced more by the individuals who are neither comfortable nor uncomfortable with using computers.

Similarly in CWB, the sigma value is 0.000 < 0.05 showed that counter-productive work behavior was significantly not equal in all individuals and the employees who are somewhat uncomfortable with using computers are more involved in CWB.

Satisfied with internet skills

Table 83

	satisfied with internet skills	N	Mean Rank	Sigma value
Variable 1: Job Stress	Very satisfied	160	163.91	
	somewhat satisfied	112	182.13	
	Neither satisfied nor unsatisfied	46	211.23	0.065
	Somewhat unsatisfied	21	159.76	
	Very unsatisfied	13	187.12	
	Total	352		
Variable 2: CWB	Very satisfied	160	156.81	
	somewhat satisfied	112	174.97	
	Neither satisfied nor unsatisfied	46	217.65	0.001
	Somewhat unsatisfied	21	227.48	
	Very unsatisfied	13	204.04	
	Total	352		

In Kruskal Wallis test for individuals internet skills, the sigma value for job stress is $0.065 > 0.05$ showed that stress was significantly equal in all individuals.

Similarly in CWB, the sigma value is $0.001 < 0.05$ showed that counter-productive work behavior was significantly not equal in all individuals having different level of internet skills. Moreover the CWB is greater in employees who are somewhat unsatisfied with their internet skills.

Mann-Whitney Test on Job Stress

Table 84

No.	Test Variables	Grouping Variables	Mean Ranks		Z-value	P-value
			Male	Female		
1	Huge attention	Gender	172.82	189.86	-1.446	0.148
2	Remember things	Gender	174.13	185.1	-0.88	0.374
3	Excessive Workload	Gender	172.81	189.91	-1.354	0.176
4	Poor Communication	Gender	172.72	190.24	-1.367	0.172
5	Unclear Roles	Gender	167.05	210.8	-3.3443	0.001
6	Conflicts between staff	Gender	171.75	193.76	-1.720	0.085
7	Not receive appreciation	Gender	177.41	173.21	-0.329	0.742
8	Unfair performance evaluation system	Gender	175.07	181.7	-0.521	0.603
9	No opportunities of advancement	Gender	173.36	187.89	-1.146	0.252
10	Technology problems	Gender	173.17	186.41	-1.044	0.296
11	Age Problems	Gender	174.79	182.72	-0.633	0.527
12	Noisy Area	Gender	181.52	158.28	-1.832	0.067
13	No emotional attachment	Gender	182.53	154.59	-2.201	0.028

14	Boss shouting	Gender	177.85	171.59	-0.498	0.618
15	Leg pullying behavior	Gender	178.63	168.78	-0.776	0.438
16	Long working hours	Gender	178.88	167.87	-0.864	0.387
17	Unsatisfied with salary	Gender	181.51	158.32	-1.812	0.7
18	Boring and dull workplace	Gender	179.90	164.16	-1.244	0.213
19	Overtime	Gender	180.04	163.64	-1.290	0.197

1. The p-value for huge attention is 0.148 > 0.05 showed that huge attention given to work was significantly equal in males and females.

2. The p-value for remember many things is 0.374 > 0.05 showed that remember many things in job was significantly equal in males and females.

3. The p-value for excessive workload is 0.176 > 0.05 showed that excessive workload was significantly equal in males and females.

4. The p-value for poor communication is 0.172 > 0.05 showed that poor communication in workplace was significantly equal faced by males and females.

5. The p-value for unclear roles and responsibilities is 0.001 < 0.05 showed that unclear roles and responsibilities was significantly not equal in males and females. Furthermore the mean ranks depict that females have more unclear roles and responsibilities than males.

6. The p-value for conflict between staff members is 0.085 > 0.05 showed that conflicts between staff was significantly equal in males and females.

7. The p-value for not receive any appreciation is 0.742 > 0.05 showed that appreciation given to employees when their work is good was significantly equal in males and females.

8. The p-value for unfair performance evaluation system is 0.603 > 0.05 showed that results on organization unfair performance evaluation system was significantly equal in males and females.

9. The p-value for no opportunities for advancement is 0.252 > 0.05 showed that opportunities for advancement was significantly equal in males and females.

10. The technology problems p-value is 0.296 > 0.05 showed that both males and females have faced the same technological problems.

11. The age problems p-value is 0.527 > 0.05 showed that aging problems was significantly equal in males and females.

12. The noisy area p-value is 0.067 > 0.05 showed that both males and females have equally faced the problem of noisy working area.

13. The emotional attachment p-value is 0.0.028 < 0.05 showed that emotional attachment with work was significantly not equal in males and females. Furthermore it is evident that males have felt it more as compared to females.

14. The boss shouting p-value is 0.618 > 0.05 showed that shouting faced by boss was significantly equal in males and females.

15. The leg pullying behavior p-value is 0.438 > 0.05 showed that leg pullying behavior faced by males and females was significantly equal.

16. The long working hour's p-value is 0.387 > 0.05 showed that long working hours in workplace was significantly equal in males and females.

17. The salary rewards p-value is 0.70 > 0.05 showed that dissatisfaction with salary rewards was significantly equal in males and females.

18. The boring and dull workplace p-value is 0.213 > 0.05 showed that it was significantly equal in males and females.

19. The overtime problems p-value is 0.197 > 0.05 showed that work overtime due to pressure of work was significantly equal in males and females.

Correlation Analysis

Correlation between job stress and its impact on employees CWB

Table 85

		Variable 1: Job Stress	**Variable 2: CWB**
Variable 1: Job Stress	Pearson Correlation	1	**.379**
	Sig. (2-tailed)		**.000**
	N	352	352
Variable 2: CWB	Pearson Correlation	**.379**	1
	Sig. (2-tailed)	**.000**	
	N	352	352

Correlation is significant at the 0.01 level (2-tailed).

In the correlation table we get Pearson correlation coefficient and sigma (2-tailed) p-value of both the variables. The sigma value is 0.000 means that there is a relationship between job stress and CWB and the degree between job stress and CWB is 37.9%.

From the value of correlation coefficient it is concluded that there is not a strong but still a sufficient positive correlation between job stress and CWB exists.

Regression Analysis

Figure: 4

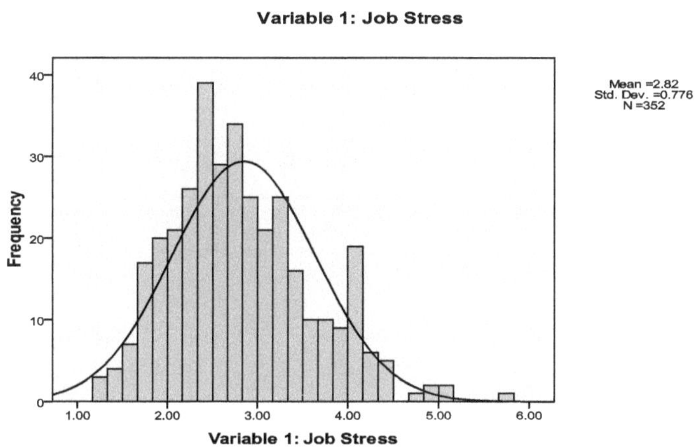

Figure: 5

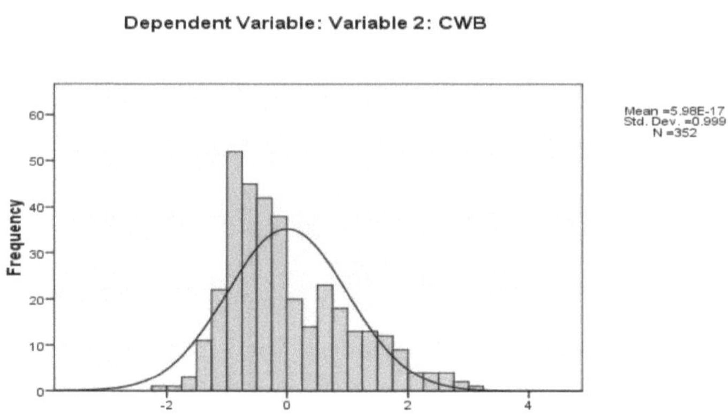

The histogram of the dependent variable is normal and we can run regression on it.

Table 86

Model Summary

Model	R	R Square	Adjusted R Square	Std. Error of the Estimate
1	.379[a]	.144	.141	.67669

In the model summary generated by SPSS, the "R" shows the correlation between both variables, "R square" tells the level of association between both the variables and adjusted R square tells the level of association within population.

The value of adjusted R square is 0.141 or 14.1% means that 14.1% employees involved in counter-productive work behavior due to work stress.

Table 87

Coefficients

Model		Unstandardized Coefficients		Standardized Coefficients	t	Sig.
		B	Std. Error	Beta		
1	(Constant)	.747	.136		5.473	.000
	Variable 1: Job Stress	.359	.047	.379	7.668	.000

a. Dependent Variable: Variable 2: CWB

The p-value for beta coefficient of variable 1: job stress was 0.000. Therefore we cannot accept the null hypothesis.

The impact of job stress was positively related with employee CWB.

Discussion

While a number of studies in job stress literature have demonstrated that job stressor lead to negative behavior such as CWB.

The purpose of the current study is to examine the relationship between job stress and CWB. On the basis of survey results there are total 78.4% males and 21.6% females. It is seen that the value of chronbach alpha for job stress, CWB and questionnaire is greater than 0.7 which shows that the questions on job stress and CWB are reliable.

The results shows that overall sample is facing job stress mainly due to huge deal of attention demanded by their work beyond normal jobs range, remember many things, excessive workload than normal work, forced to work more by their supervisors and employers, poor communication, no appreciation received from management, unfair performance evaluation system, inappropriate working conditions and inappropriate salaries and rewards. These all job stressors lead the employee towards CWB. The major CWB in which the employees are involved due to job stress as shown by the survey results are purposely damaged their organization property, come to late work without permission, stayed at home to avoid work and purposely work incorrectly. Although the percentage of employees involved in CWB due to job stress is low in banking sector and most of the employees said that they are not engage in any negative behavior but still if the issue of job stress is not catered properly by the organizations than there are bright possibility that the percentage of employees involved in CWB in the future will raise.

The results also shows that male sample who have the professional experience of more than 9 years have switched their jobs most and are more job stress and most of the sample are satisfied with their computers and Internet skills. The results shows that job stress was significantly not equal in males and females and female sample is facing more job stress than males and the individuals who are more than 56 years of age bear more job stress. Similarly the individuals who are earning less than 25,000, have field jobs, live in their own houses, using bus for going to office, having dependents 5-8 and of designation OG-III are facing more job stress than the rest of the sample.

The value of Pearson correlation is 0.379 which shows that there is not strong but still enough positive correlation exists between job stress and CWB. In regression analysis the results shows that the value of adjusted R square is 0.141 or 14.1% which means that 14.1% employees involved in CWB due to job stress and also the p-value for beta coefficient was 0.000. Thus we cannot accept the null hypothesis and concluded that "There is a positive impact of job stress on employees CWB".

Conclusion

This study attempts to see the relationship between job stress and employee CWB. On the basis of survey results it is concluded that there is an impact of job stress on employees, the employees working in different banks suffered from stress and this stress somewhat lead them to counter-productive work behavior. The correlation analysis also shows that there is enough positive correlation exist between job stress and employee counter-productive work behavior. The p-value for beta coefficient in regression analysis was also 0.000, thus we reject the null hypothesis and accept the alternate hypothesis which also states that the impact of job stress was positively related with employee CWB.

Moreover, the findings from past researches also reveal the same that the employee involved in retaliatory acts such as CWB due to job stress.

Limitations and Recommendations

The limitations of this study are this study caters only the limited population and cannot take the whole view of population. Furthermore this study only includes the banking sector of Pakistan and not the other sectors. The time and financial constraints are the major limitations in this study. Lastly the tool which was used i.e. questionnaire cannot capture the non-verbal behavior of employees.

The recommendations for the next researches are that the study should be on large level which largely represents the population. Secondly the recommendation for the organizations is that there must be stress management programs in organizations and it is proved by previous researches that the organizations who have effective stress management programs, talk on regular basis with their workers and have efficient system, procedures and policies to deal with employee stress related issues like employee absence and workplace discipline are much more able to avoid stress situations and to cope up with employee problems as they arise. Lastly this study results shows that the employees feel stressed due to excessive workload, huge deal of attention given to work beyond job's range and many other factors so there is a need to resolve these issues by the organization.

- World Health Organization. (n.d.). *Stress at the workplace.* Retrieved from World Health Organization: http://www.who.int/occupational_health/topics/stressatwp/en/
- (Lyons, Hrebeniak & Alutto, & Porter & Steers,). (1971; 1972; 1973). *The role of personality, occupation and organization in understanding the relationship between job stress, performance and absenteeism.* Great Britain: Journal of Occupational Psychology.
- Aizzat Mohd Nasurdin; T. Ramayah; S. Kemaresan. *Organizational stressors and the job stress among managers: The moderating role of neuroticism.*
- Aizzat Mohd Nasurdin; T. Ramayah; S. Kemaresan. *Organizational stressors and the role among managers: The moderating role of neuroticism.*
- Aizzat Mohd Nasurdin; T. Ramayah; S. Kemaresan. *Organizational stressors and the role among managers: The moderating role of neuroticism.*
- Arsenault, A., & Dolan, S. (1983). The role of personality, occupation and organization in understanding the relationship between job stress, performance and absenteeism. *Journal of Occupational Psychology* , pp 227-240.
- Caplan, House, & Matteson, I. &. (1972; 1974; 1979). *The role of personality, occupation and organization in understanding the relationship between job stress,performance and absenteeism.* Great Britain: Journal of Occupational Psychology.
- (2003). *Enough Workplace Stress: Organizing for Change.* The Canadian Union of Public Employees.
- Greiner. (1998).
- Gruys, M. L., & Sackett, P. R. (2003). Investigating the dimensionality of counter-productive work behavior. *International journal of selection and assessment.* , pg 30-42, Volume: 11.
- Gruys, M. L., & Sakett, P. R. (2003). *Investgating the dimensionality of counter-productive work behavior.* International journal of selection and assessment.
- Hoel, Giga. (2003).

- Imtiaz, S., & Ahmad, S. (2009). Impact Of Stress On Employee Productivity, Performance And Turnover; An Important Managerial Issue. *International Review of Business Research Papers.* , Vol. 5 No. Pp. 468-477.
- Imtiaz, Subha; Ahmad, Shakil. (2009). Impact Of Stress On Employee Productivity, Performance And Turnover; An Important Managerial Issue. *International Review of Business Research Papers* , Vol. 5 No. Pp. 468-477.
- Jenkins, & Kasl. (1976; 1973,1974). *The role of personality, occupation and organization in understanding the relationship between job stress,performance and absenteeism.* Great Britain: Journal of Occupational Psycholog.
- Kennard, J. (2008). *A Brief History of the term Stress.* Retrieved from Health Central: http://www.healthcentral.com/anxiety/c/1950/30437/history-term-stress
- Kim, J., Sorhaindo, B., & Garman, E. T. (2006). *Relationship between Financial Stress and Workplace. Absenteeism of Credit Counseling Clients.* Springer Science+Business Media, Inc.
- Klink, v. d., & al., e. (2001). *Work-related Stress in Division of Youth and Family Caseworkers: Determining Whether a Cognitive Behavioral Intervention Will Decrease Stress.* Retrieved from URC: http://www.kon.org/urc/v7/purdy.html
- Klink, v. d., Blonk, Scheme, & Dijk, v. (2001). *Work-related Stress in Division of Youth and Family Caseworkers: Determining Whether a Cognitive Behavioral Intervention Will Decrease Stress.* . Retrieved from URC: http://www.kon.org/urc/v7/purdy.html
- Lee, D. (1997). *Employee Stress: The True Cost.* Retrieved from Human Nature at Work: http://www.humannatureatwork.com/Workplace-Stress-1.htm
- Lu, Luo. (1999). Work Motivation, Job Stress and Employees Well-being. *Journal of Applied Management Studies.* , Vol. 8, No. 1 pg. 61-72.
- Mansoor, M., Fida, S., Nasir, S., & Ahmad, Z. (2011). The Impact of Job Stress on Employee Job Satisfaction. A Study on Telecommunication Sector of Pakistan. *Journal of Business Studies Quarterly* , Vol. 2, No. 3, pp. 50-56.

- Mansoor, Muhammad; Fida, Sabtain; Nasir, Saima; Ahmad, Zubair. (2011). The Impact of Job Stress on Employee Job Satisfaction. A Study on Telecommunication Sector of Pakistan. *Journal of Business Studies Quarterly* , Vol. 2, No. 3, pp. 50-56.

- Mansoor, Muhammad; Fida, Sabtain; Nasir, Saima; Ahmad, Zubair. (2011). The Impact of Job Stress on Employee Job Satisfaction. A Study on Telecommunication Sector of Pakistan. *Journal of Business Studies Quarterly* , Vol. 2, No. 3, pp. 50-56.

- Mansoor, Muhammad; Fida, Sabtain; Nasir, Saima; Ahmad, Zubair. (2004). The Impact of Job Stress on Employee Job Satisfaction. A Study on Telecommunication Sector of Pakistan. *Journal of Business Studies Quarterly* , Vol. 2, No. 3, pp. 50-56.

- Mansoor, Muhammad; Fida, Sabtain; Nasir, Saima; Ahmad, Zubair. (2011). The Impact of Job Stress on Employee Job Satisfaction. A Study on Telecommunication Sector of Pakistan. *Journal of Business Studies Quarterly.* , Vol. 2, No. 3, pp. 50-56.

- Mansoor, Muhammad; Fida, Sabtain; Nasir, Saima; Ahmad., Zubair. (2011). The Impact of Job Stress on Employee Job Satisfaction. A Study on Telecommunication Sector of Pakistan. *Journal of Business Studies Quarterly* , Vol. 2, No. 3, pp. 50-56.

- Meneze. (2005).

- Meneze. (2005). *Impact Of Stress On Employee Productivity, Performance And Turnover; An Important Managerial Issue.* Retrieved from Academia.edu: http://ciit-isb.academia.edu/MuhammadShakilAhmad/Papers/263254/The_Impact_of_Stress_on_Employee_Productivity_Performance_and_Turn_over_an_important_managerial_issue

- Mojoyinola, J. K. (2008). *Effects of Job Stress on Health, Personal and Work Behaviour of Nurses in Public Hospitals in Ibadan Metropolis, Nigeria.* Ethno-Med., 2(2): 143-148.

- Mojoyinola, J. K. (2008). *Effects of Job Stress on Health, Personal and Work Behaviour of Nurses in Public Hospitals in Ibadan Metropolis, Nigeria.* Ethno-Med., 2(2): 143-148.

- Muhammad Mansoor; Sabtain Fida; Saima Nasir; Zubair Ahmad. (2011). The Impact of Job Stress on Employee Job Satisfaction. A Study on Telecommunication Sector of Pakistan. *Journal of Business Studies Quarterly* , Vol. 2, No. 3, pp. 50-56.
- Nasurdin, A. M., Ramayah, T., & Kemaresan, S. *Organizational Stressors And Job Stress Among Managers: The Moderating Role Of Neuroticism.*
- NIOSH - U.S. Department of Health and Services. *Stress at Work.* US: Publications Dissemination, EID National Institute for Occupational Safety and Health.
- NIOSH - U.S. Department of Health and Services. *Stress At Work.* US: Publications Dissemination, EID National Institute for Occupational Safety and Health.
- NIOSH: stress at work. (2010). *stress at work.*
- Paillé, P. (2011). Stressful Work, Citizenship Behaviour and Intention to Leave the Organization in a High Turnover Environment: Examining the Mediating Role of Job Satisfaction. *Journal of Management Research.* , Vol. 3, No. 1: pp 1-14.
- Paillé, P. (2011). Stressful Work, Citizenship Behaviour and Intention to Leave the Organization in a High Turnover Environment: Examining the Mediating Role of Job Satisfaction. *Journal of Management Research.* , Vol. 3, No. 1: pp 1-14.
- Paul. (n.d.).
- Penney, L. M., & Spector, P. E. (2005). Job stress, incivility, and counterproductive work behavior (CWB): the moderating role of negative affectivity. *Journal of Organizational Behavior* , pp 777–796.
- Pervez, A. (25th feb, 2011). *Pakistan Banking Sector.* Business Network Switzerland.
- Research roundup: Work stress. (2010, July). *Research roundup: Work stress.* Retrieved 2011, from Practice Central.: http://www.apapracticecentral.org/update/2010/07-28/research-roundup.aspx
- Sanvee. (2009). *Stress (Pressure Tension).*
- (1999). *The Office of Radiation, Chemical and Biological Safety.*

- Trevor. (2002).
- Walonick, D. S. (1993). *Causes and Cures of Stress in Organizations*. Retrieved from http://statpac.org/walonick/organizational-stress.htm
- Westman. (2005).
- *Working together to reduce stress at work. A guide for employees.* (2008, November). Retrieved 2011, from Health and Safety Executive (HSE).: http://www.hse.gov.uk/pubns/indg424.pdf
- *Workplace Stress - General*. (2008, September). Retrieved November 2011, from Canadian Centre for Occupational Health and Safety: http://www.ccohs.ca/oshanswers/psychosocial/stress.html

Appendix A

Demographics Graphs

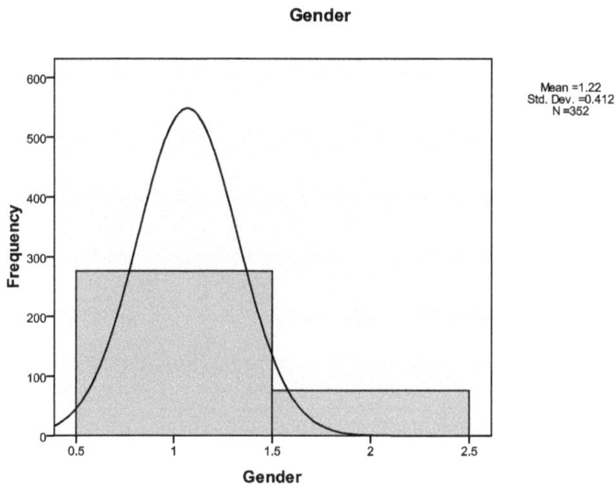

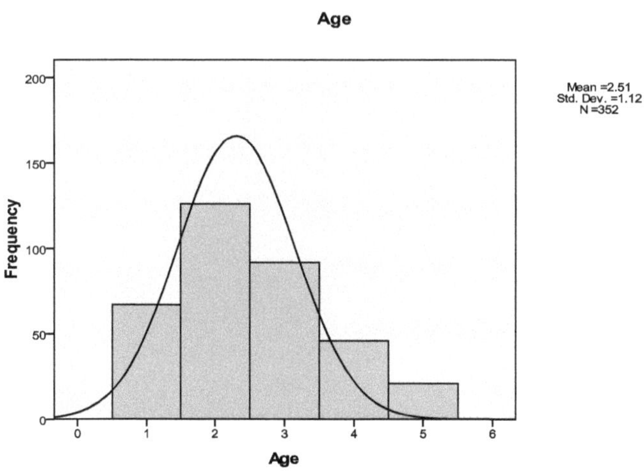

Monthly Salary

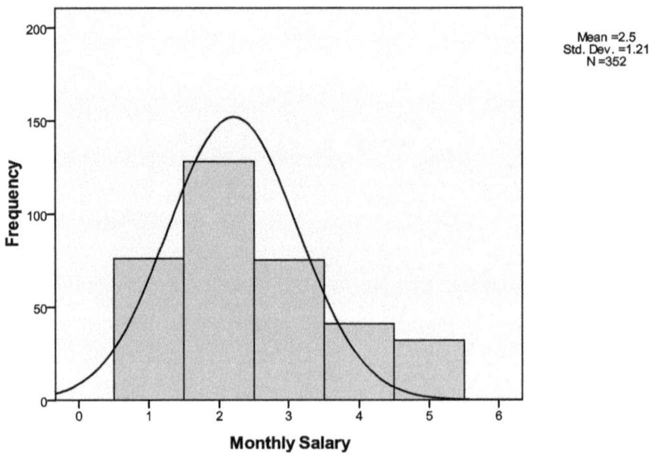

Doing this job for

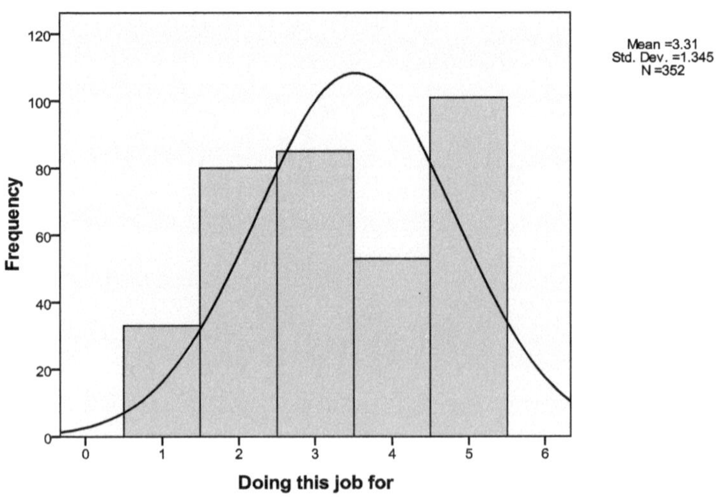

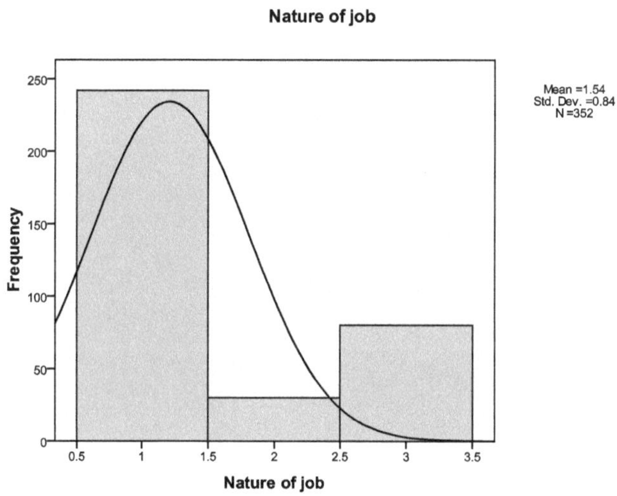
Nature of job
Frequency
250
200
150
100
50
0
0.5
1
1.5
2
2.5
3
3.5
Nature of job
Mean =1.54
Std. Dev. =0.84
N =352

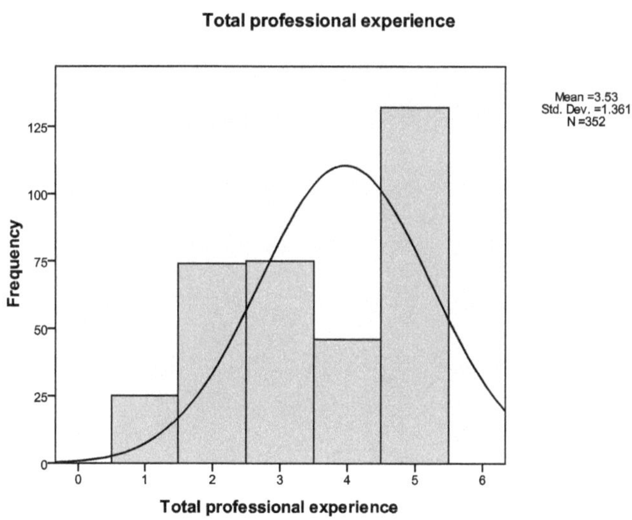
Total professional experience
Frequency
125
100
75
50
25
0
0
1
2
3
4
5
6
Total professional experience
Mean =3.53
Std. Dev. =1.361
N =352

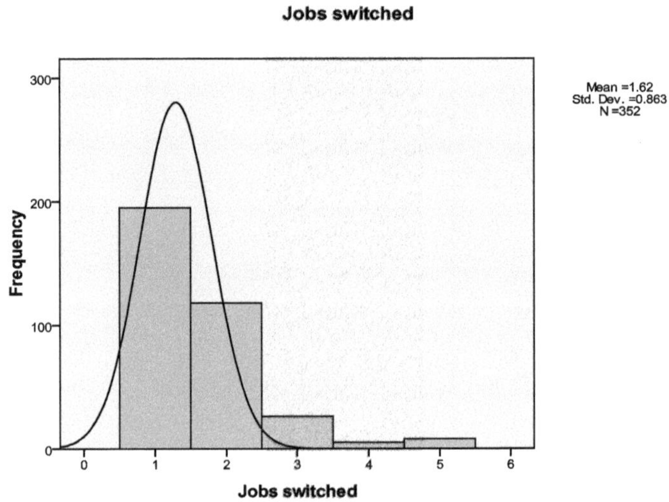
Jobs switched
Mean =1.62
Std. Dev. =0.863
N =352
Frequency
300
200
100
0
0
1
2
3
4
5
6
Jobs switched

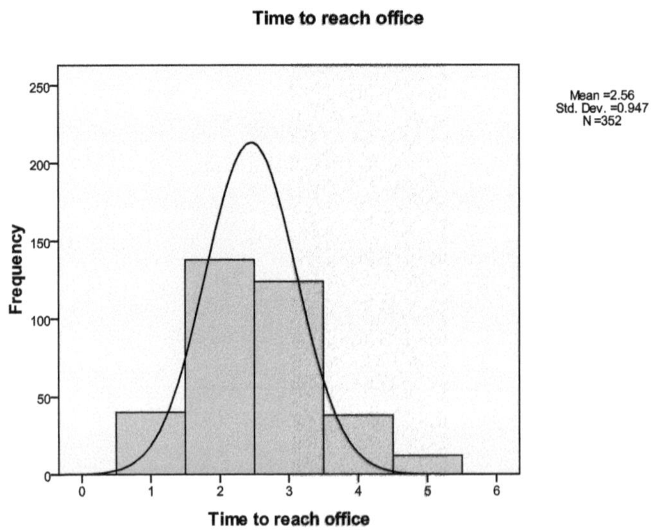
Time to reach office
Mean =2.56
Std. Dev. =0.947
N =352
Frequency
250
200
150
100
50
0
0
1
2
3
4
5
6
Time to reach office

Nature of family

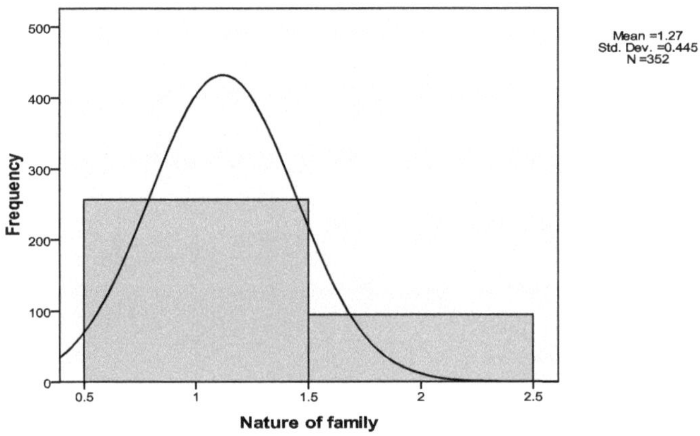

House in which live in

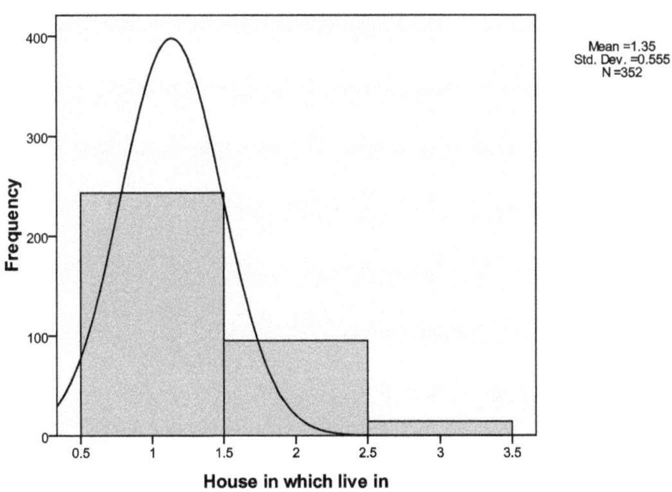

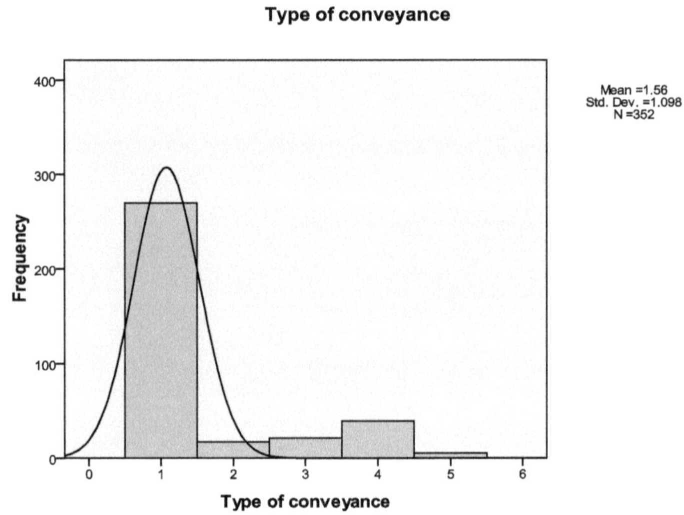
Type of conveyance
Frequency
400
300
200
100
0
0
1
2
3
4
5
6
Type of conveyance
Mean =1.56
Std. Dev. =1.098
N =352

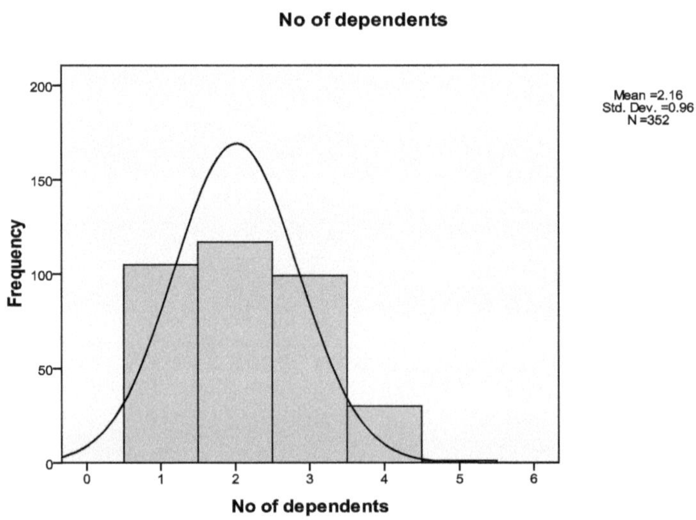
No of dependents
Frequency
200
150
100
50
0
0
1
2
3
4
5
6
No of dependents
Mean =2.16
Std. Dev. =0.96
N =352

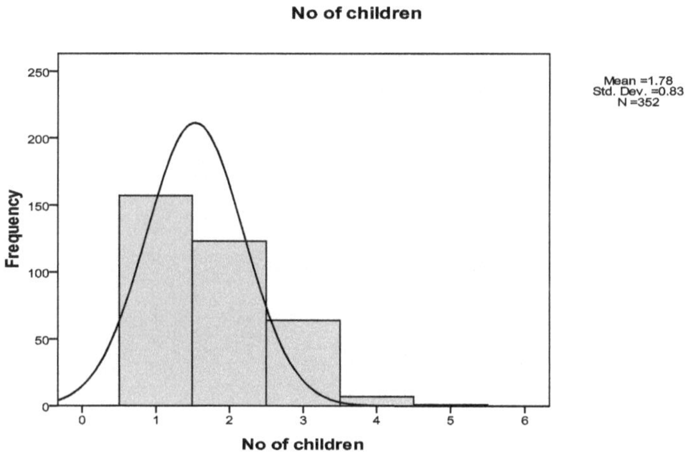
No of children
Mean =1.78
Std. Dev. =0.83
N =352
Frequency
250
200
150
100
50
0
0
1
2
3
4
5
6
No of children

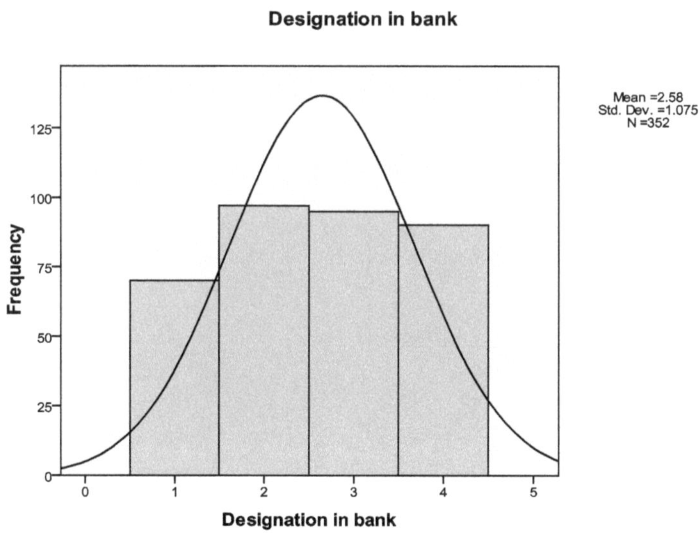
Designation in bank
Mean =2.58
Std. Dev. =1.075
N =352
Frequency
125
100
75
50
25
0
0
1
2
3
4
5
Designation in bank

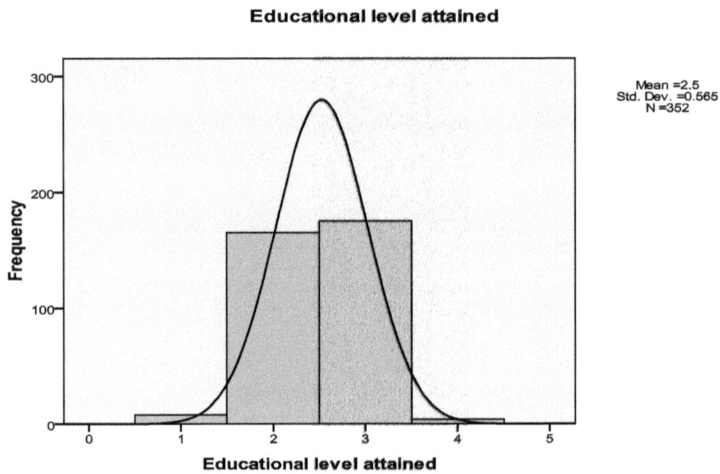
Educational level attained
Mean =2.5
Std. Dev. =0.565
N =352
Frequency
300
200
100
0
0
1
2
3
4
5
Educational level attained

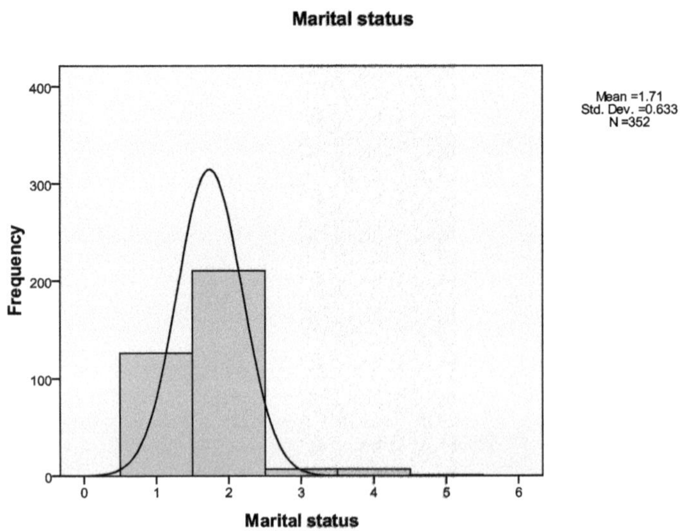
Marital status
Mean =1.71
Std. Dev. =0.633
N =352
Frequency
400
300
200
100
0
0
1
2
3
4
5
6
Marital status

Comfortable using computers

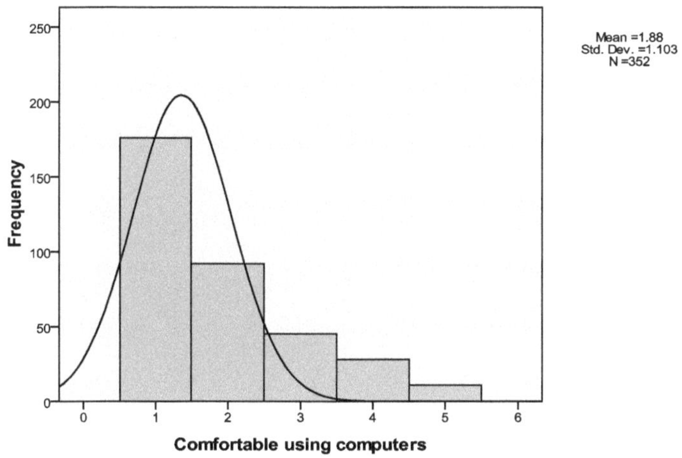

satisfied with internet skills

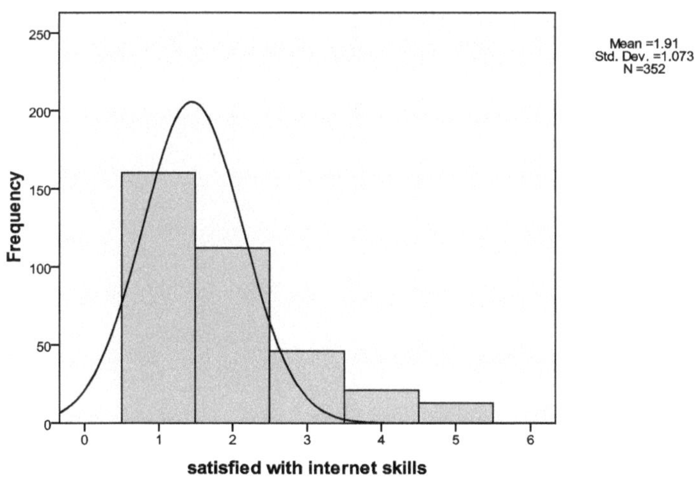

Job Stress Graphs

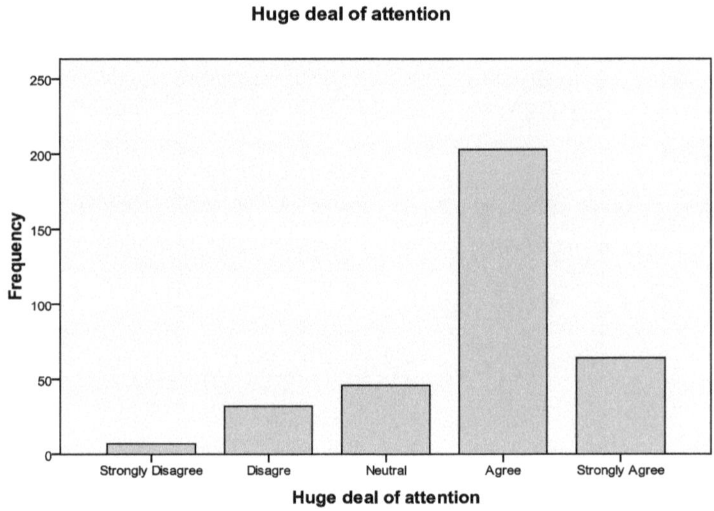

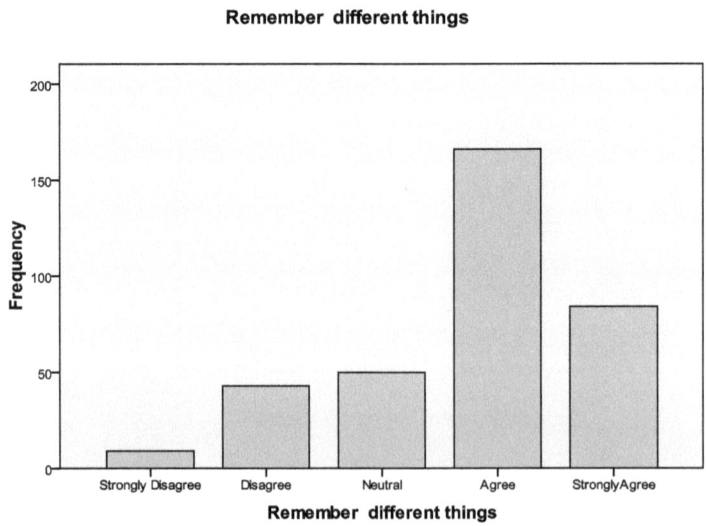

excessive workload than normal

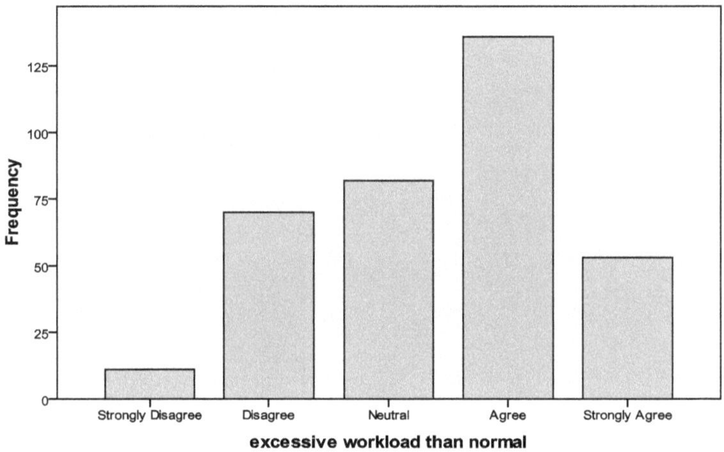

Could not finish work in work day

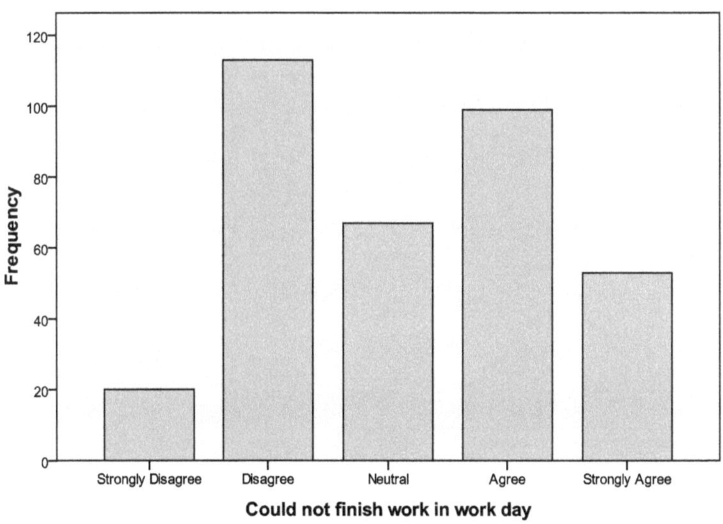

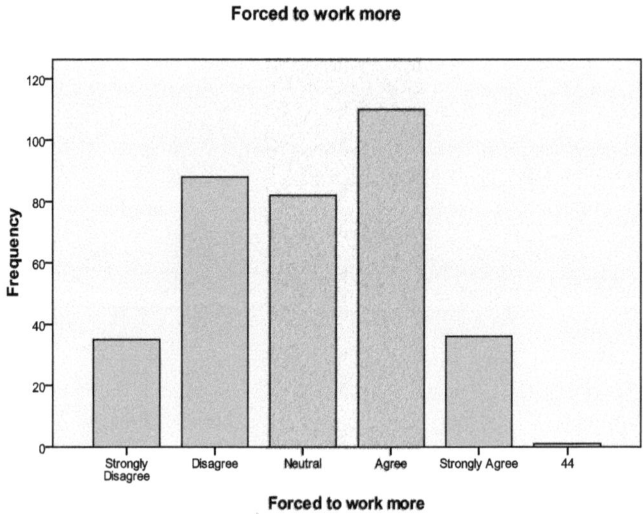
Forced to work more
120
100
80
60
40
20
0
Frequency
Strongly Disagree
Disagree
Neutral
Agree
Strongly Agree
44
Forced to work more

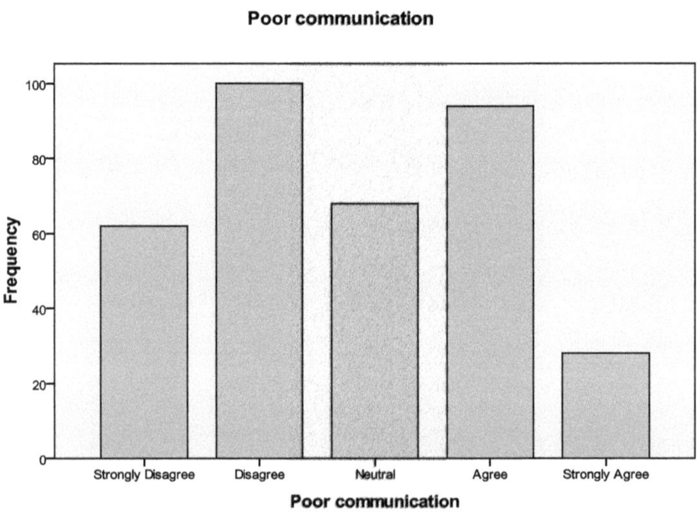
Poor communication
100
80
60
40
20
0
Frequency
Strongly Disagree
Disagree
Neutral
Agree
Strongly Agree
Poor communication

Unclear responsibilities and roles

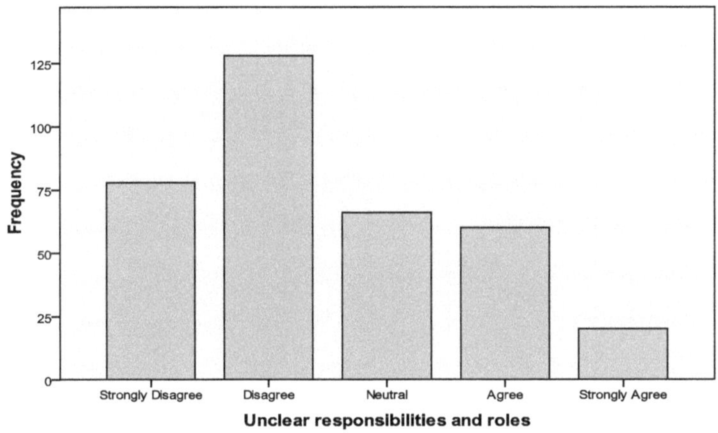

Conflicts in staff members

Not recieve any appreciation

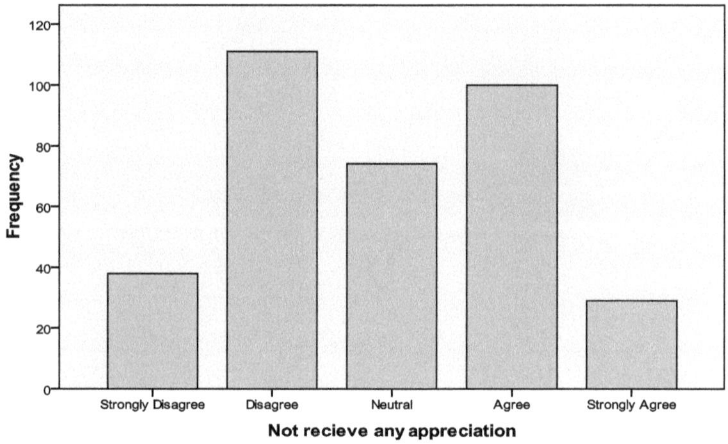

Unfair performance evaluation system

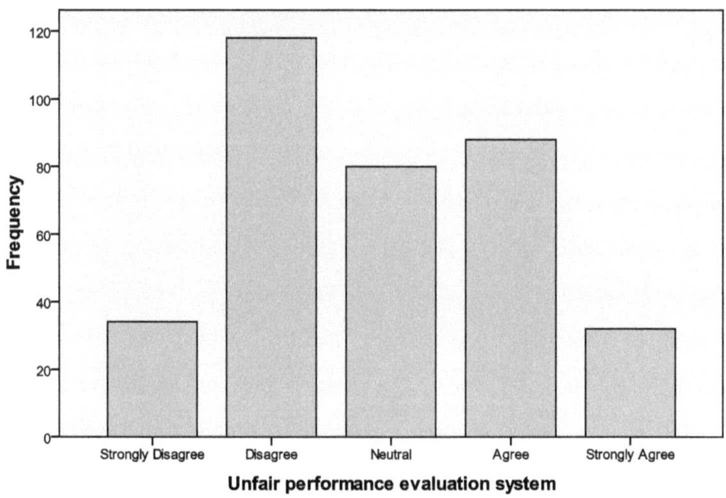

No opprotunities for advancement

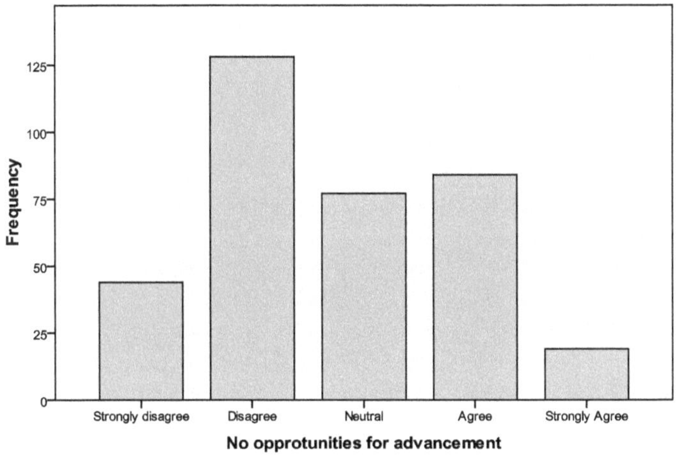

Technological problems

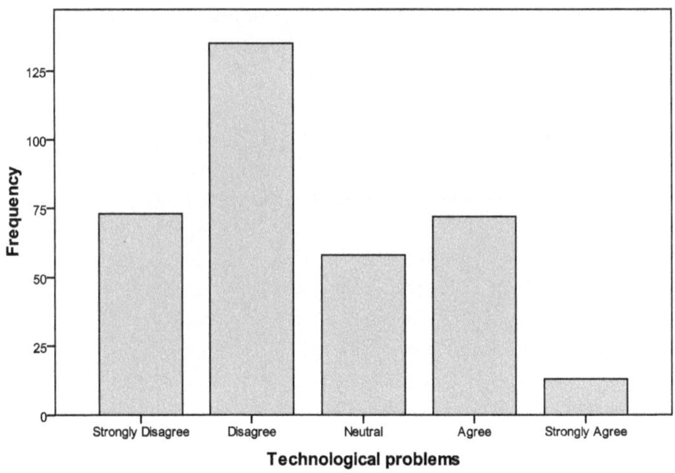

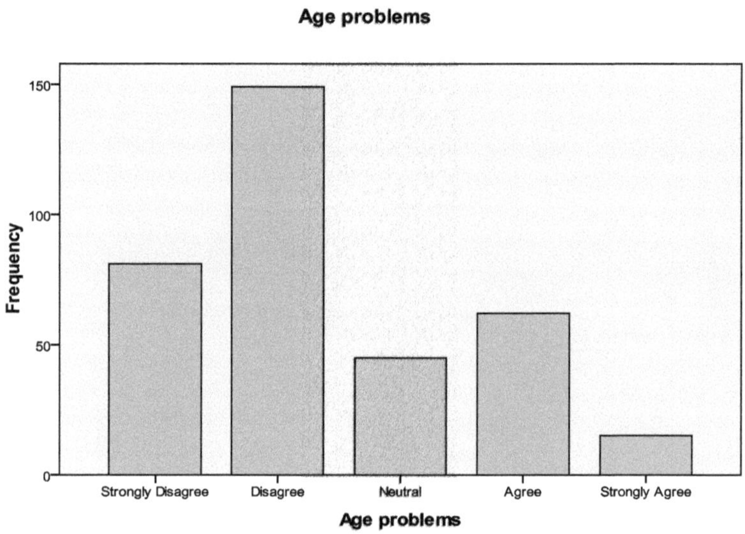
Age problems
150
100
50
0
Frequency
Strongly Disagree
Disagree
Neutral
Agree
Strongly Agree
Age problems

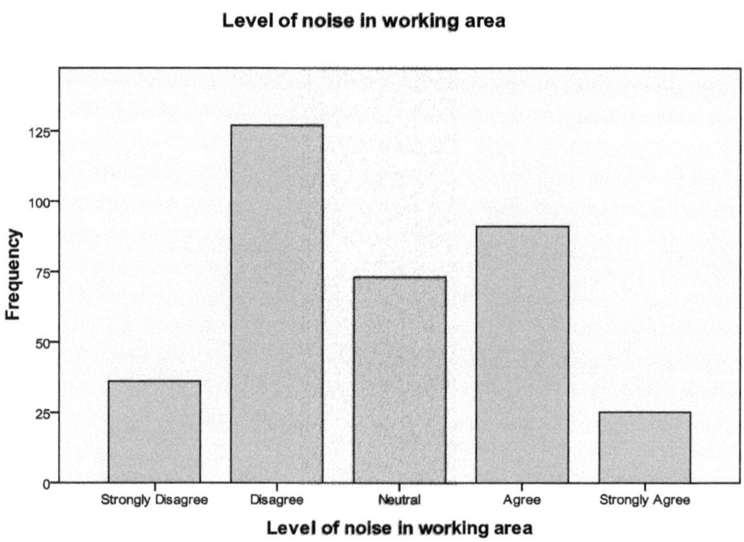
Level of noise in working area
125
100
75
50
25
0
Frequency
Strongly Disagree
Disagree
Neutral
Agree
Strongly Agree
Level of noise in working area

Extermely crowded area

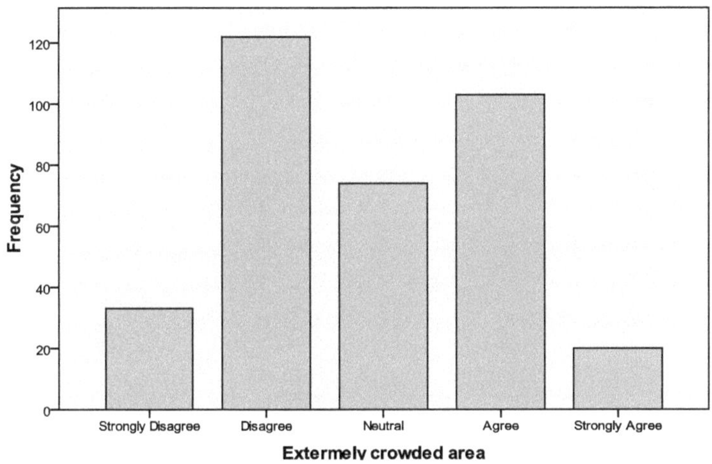

Pressure of boss to work more

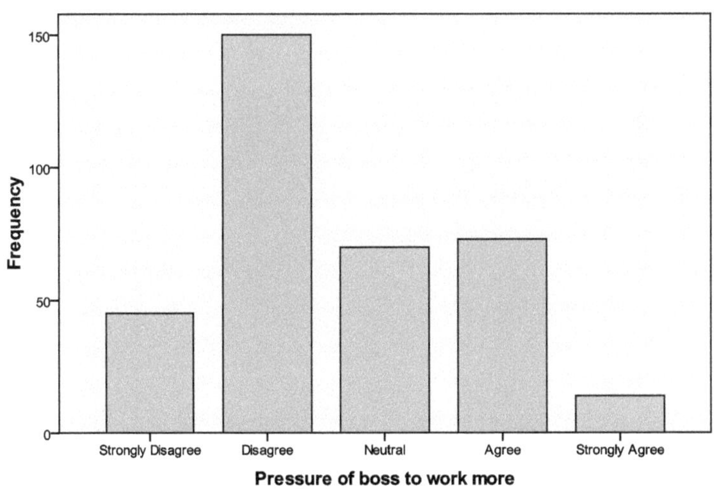

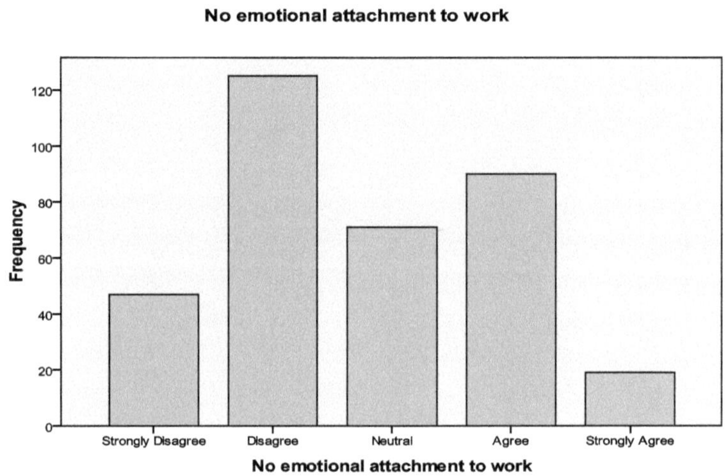
No emotional attachment to work
Frequency
120
100
80
60
40
20
0
Strongly Disagree
Disagree
Neutral
Agree
Strongly Agree
No emotional attachment to work

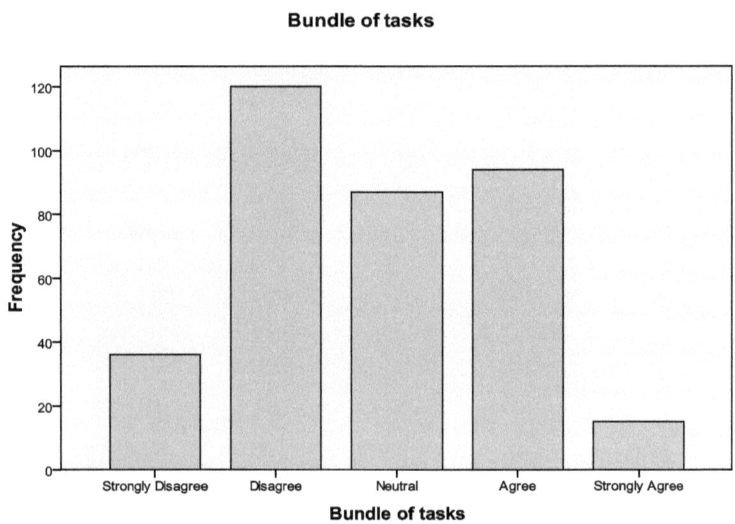
Bundle of tasks
Frequency
120
100
80
60
40
20
0
Strongly Disagree
Disagree
Neutral
Agree
Strongly Agree
Bundle of tasks

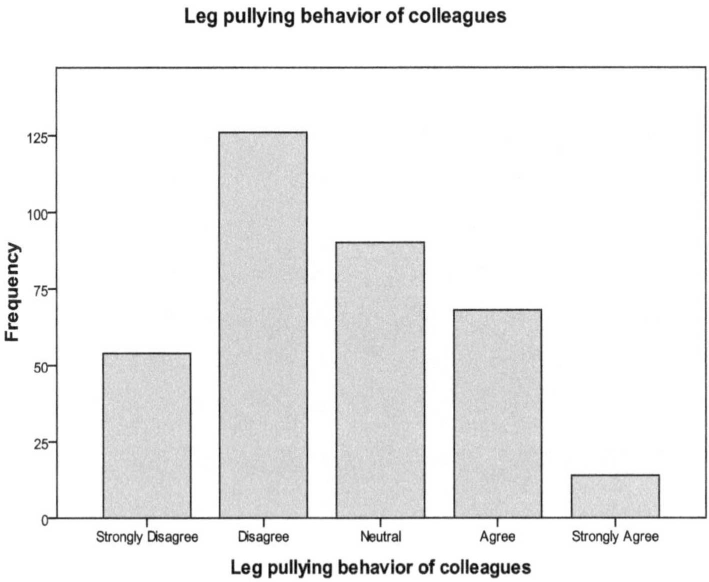
Leg pullying behavior of colleagues
Frequency
125
100
75
50
25
0
Strongly Disagree
Disagree
Neutral
Agree
Strongly Agree
Leg pullying behavior of colleagues

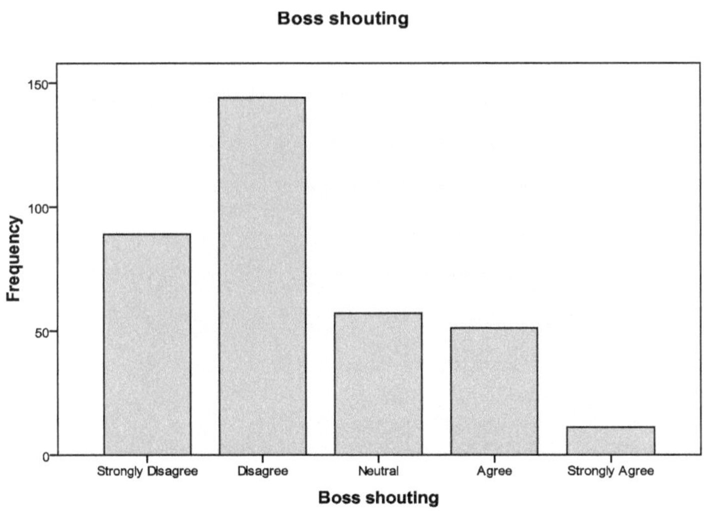
Boss shouting
Frequency
150
100
50
0
Strongly Disagree
Disagree
Neutral
Agree
Strongly Agree
Boss shouting

Uncomfortable workplace
Frequency
150
100
50
0
Strongly Disagree
Disgaree
Neutral
Agree
Strongly Agree
Uncomfortable workplace

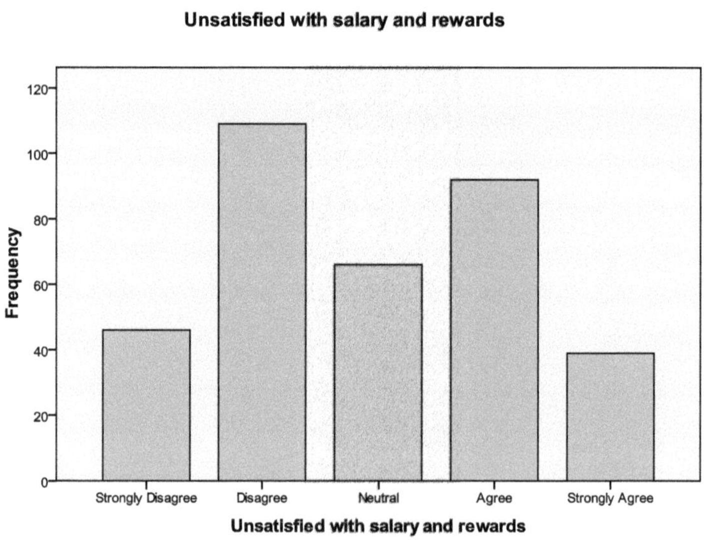
Unsatisfied with salary and rewards
Frequency
120
100
80
60
40
20
0
Strongly Disagree
Disagree
Neutral
Agree
Strongly Agree
Unsatisfied with salary and rewards

Long working hours

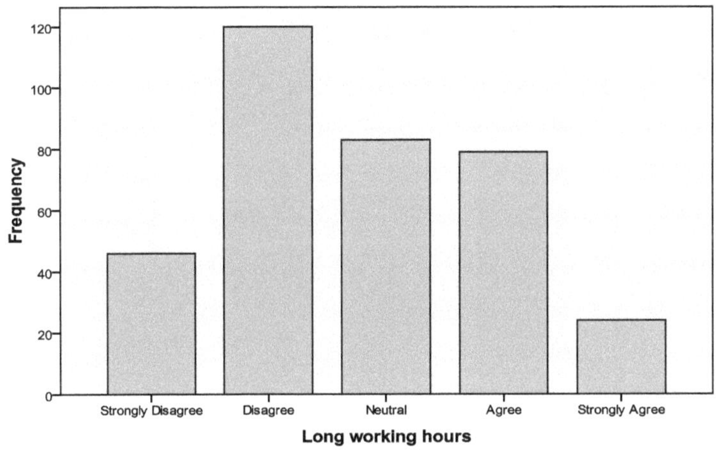

Overtime due to work pressure

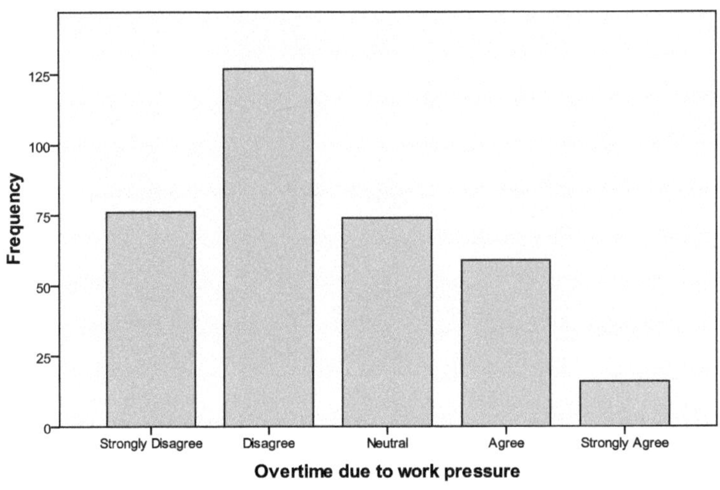

CWB Graphs

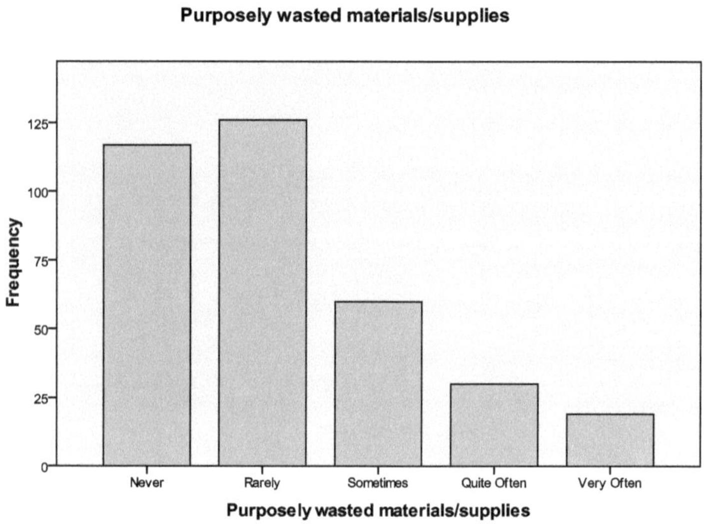
Purposely wasted materials/supplies
Frequency
125
100
75
50
25
0
Never
Rarely
Sometimes
Quite Often
Very Often
Purposely wasted materials/supplies

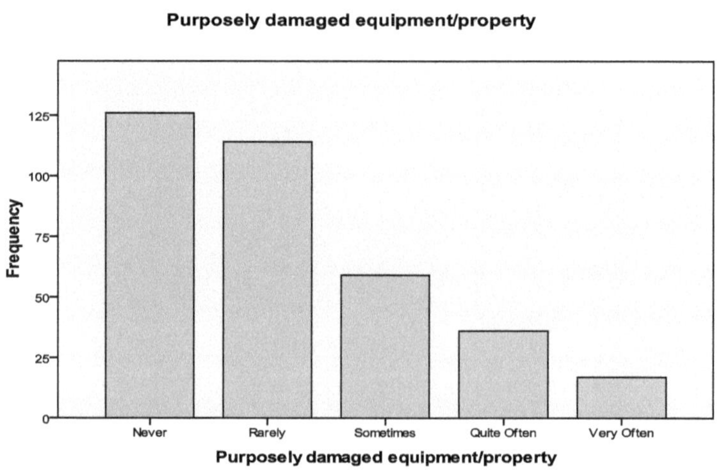
Purposely damaged equipment/property
Frequency
125
100
75
50
25
0
Never
Rarely
Sometimes
Quite Often
Very Often
Purposely damaged equipment/property

Purposely dirtied/littered workplace

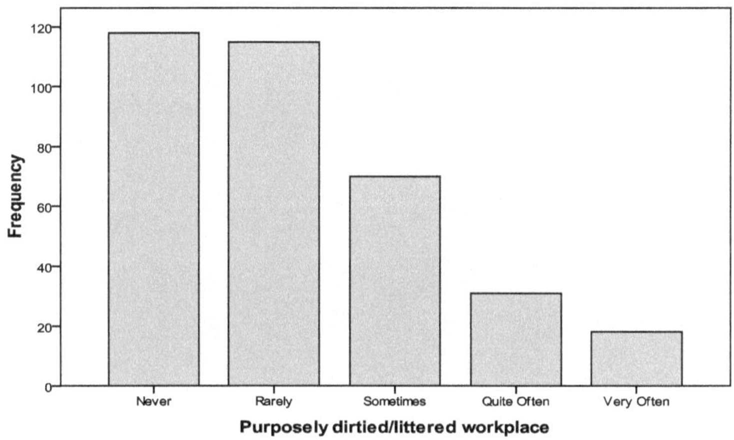

Come to work late withour permission

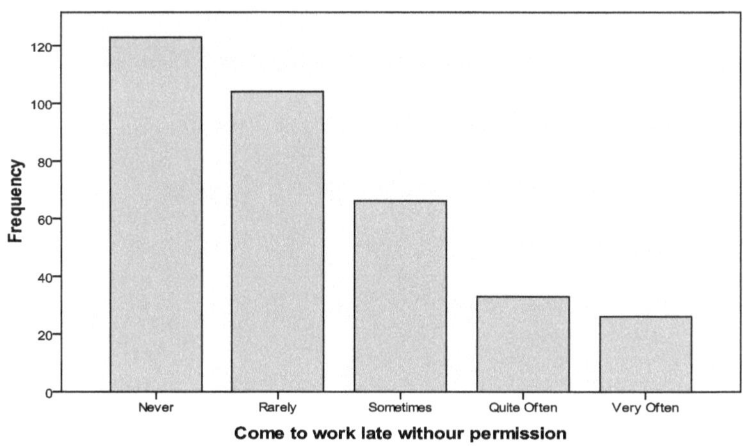

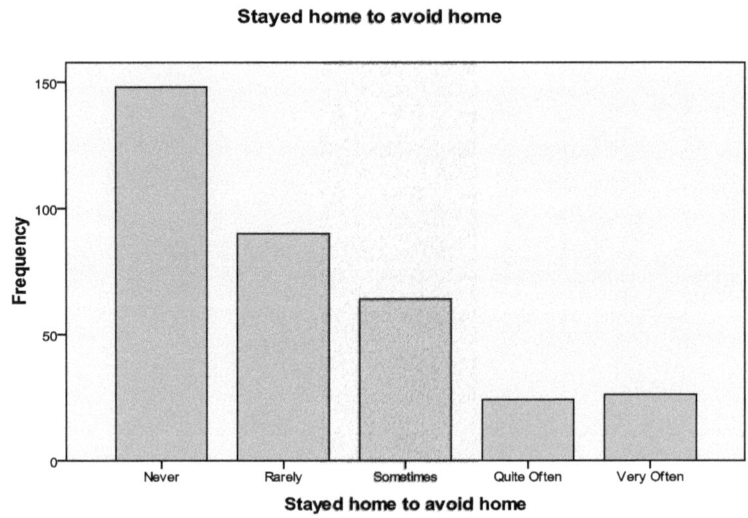
Stayed home to avoid home
150
100
50
0
Frequency
Never
Rarely
Sometimes
Quite Often
Very Often
Stayed home to avoid home

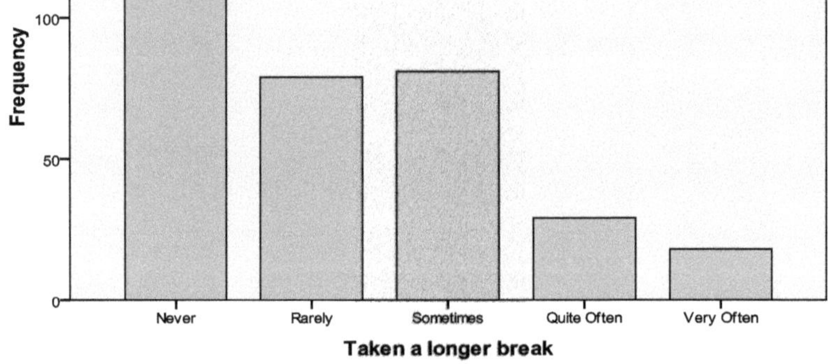
Taken a longer break
150
100
50
0
Frequency
Never
Rarely
Sometimes
Quite Often
Very Often
Taken a longer break

Left work earlier than allowed

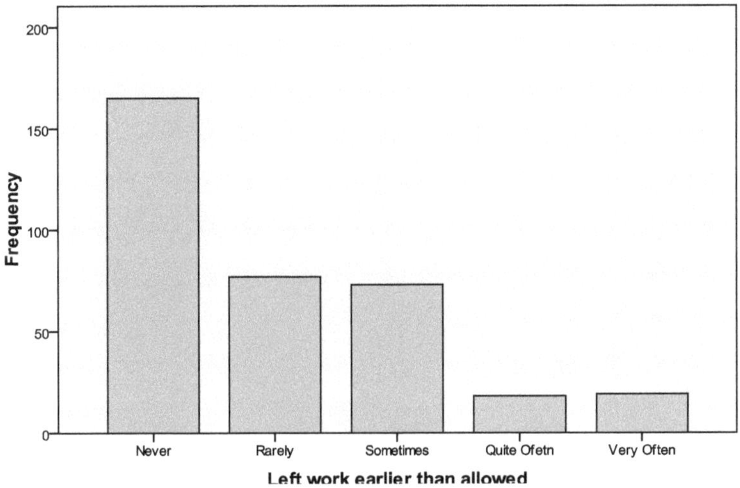

Purposely did the work incorrectly

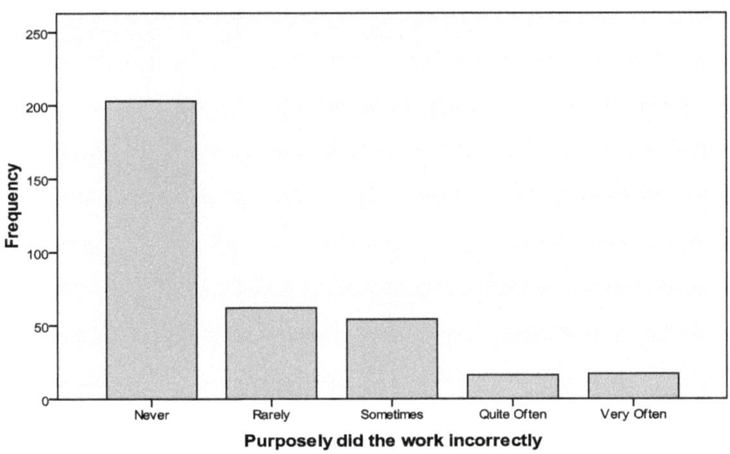

Purposely worked slowly

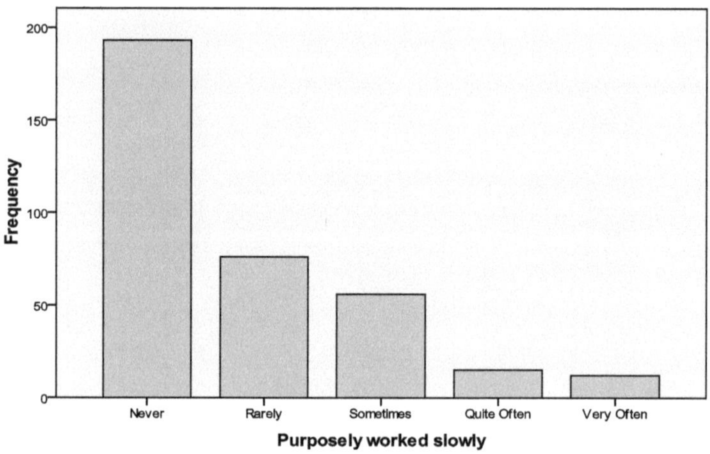

Purposely dont follow instructions

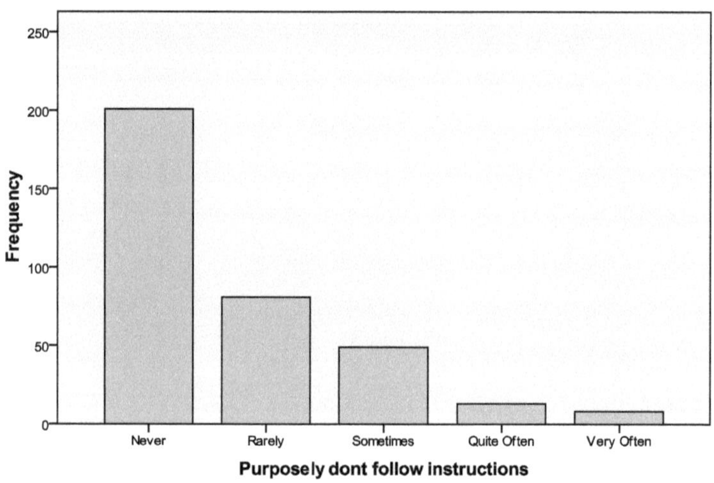

Stole something of colleagues

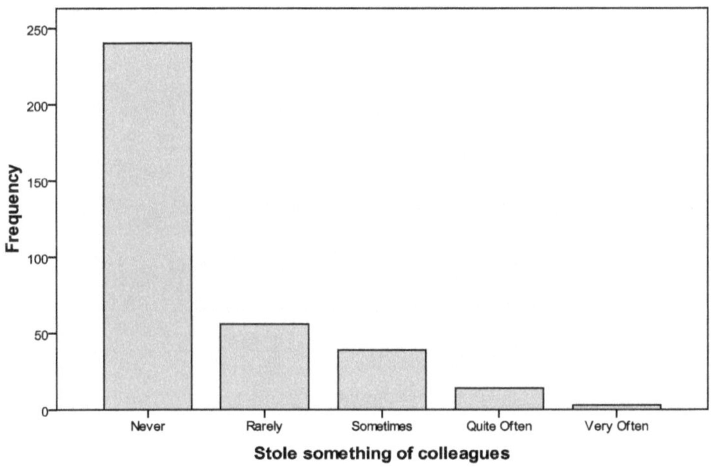

Took supplies home without permission

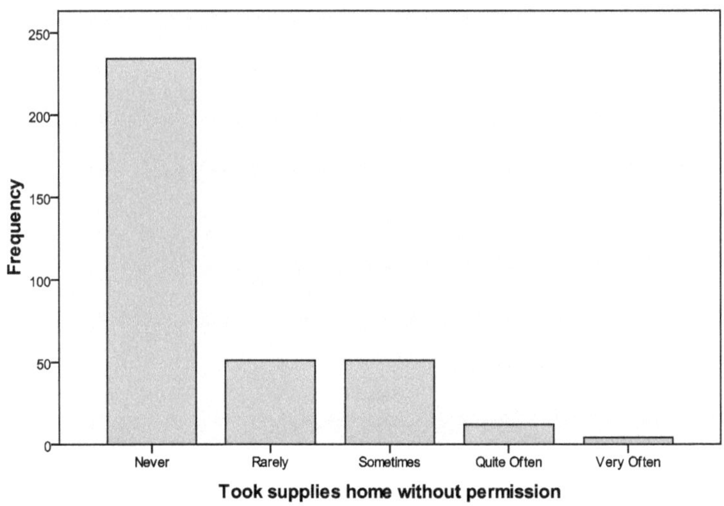

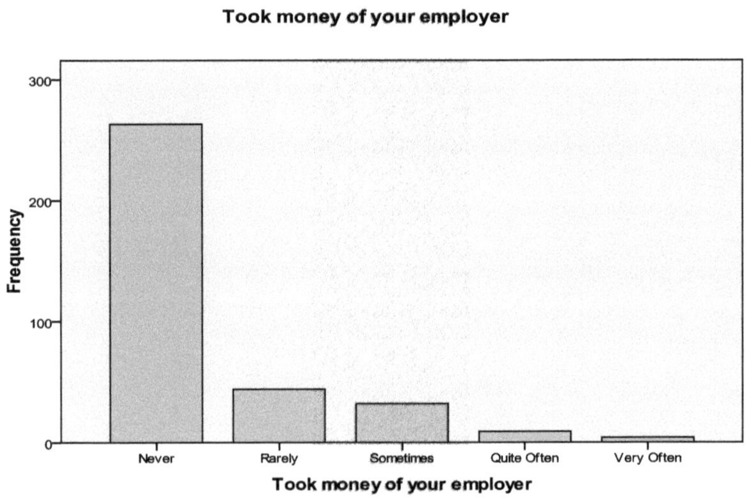
Took money of your employer
Frequency
300
200
100
0
Never
Rarely
Sometimes
Quite Often
Very Often
Took money of your employer

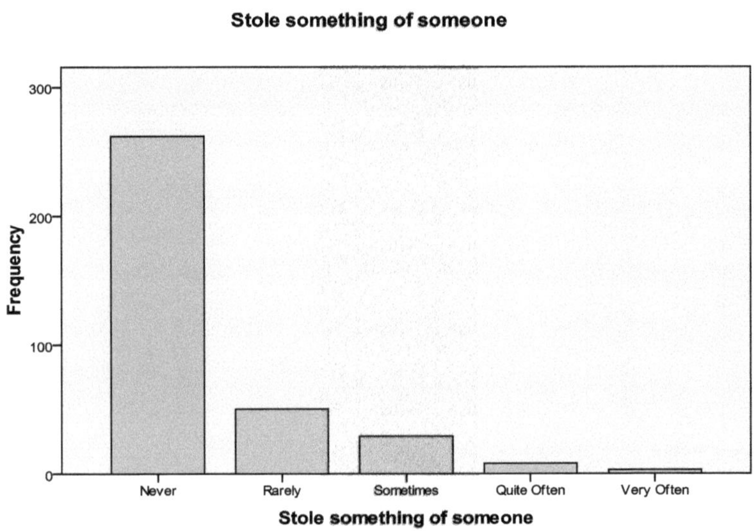
Stole something of someone
Frequency
300
200
100
0
Never
Rarely
Sometimes
Quite Often
Very Often
Stole something of someone

Been nasty or rude to customers

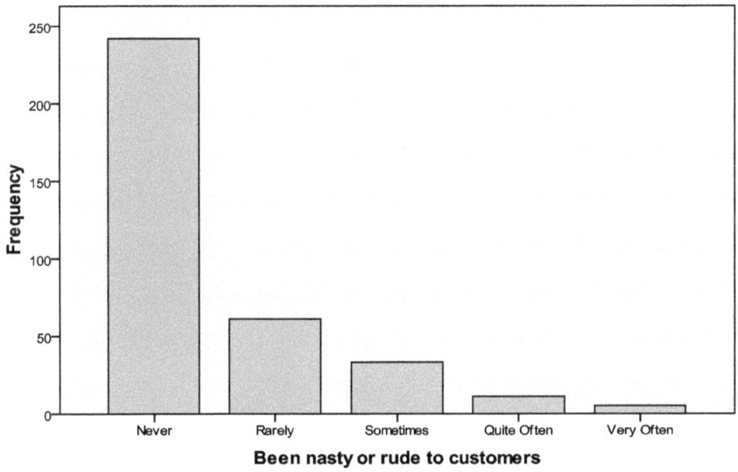

Insulted someone

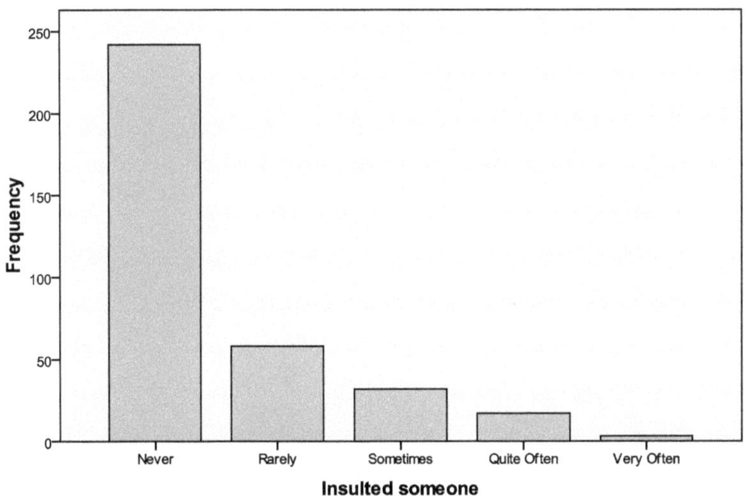

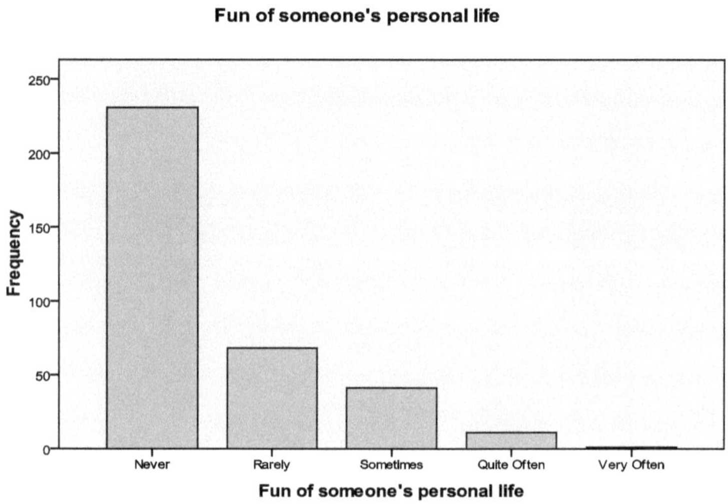
Fun of someone's personal life
Frequency
250
200
150
100
50
0
Never
Rarely
Sometimes
Quite Often
Very Often
Fun of someone's personal life

Ignored someone at work
Frequency
250
200
150
100
50
0
Never
Rarely
Sometimes
Quite Often
Very Often
Ignored someone at work

Blamed someone for error you made

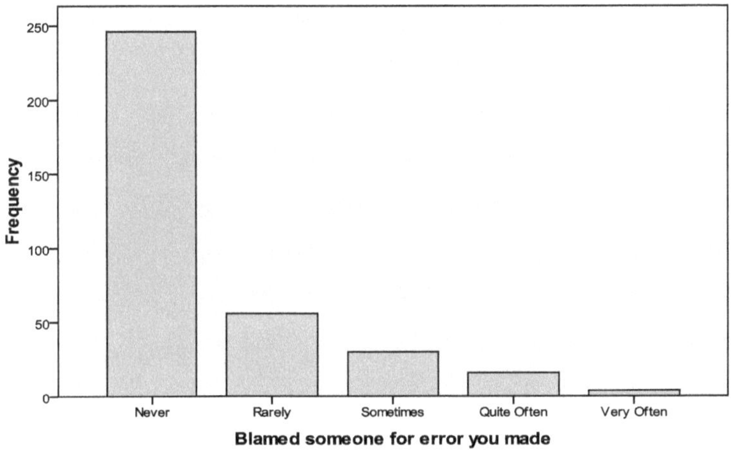

Strated an argument

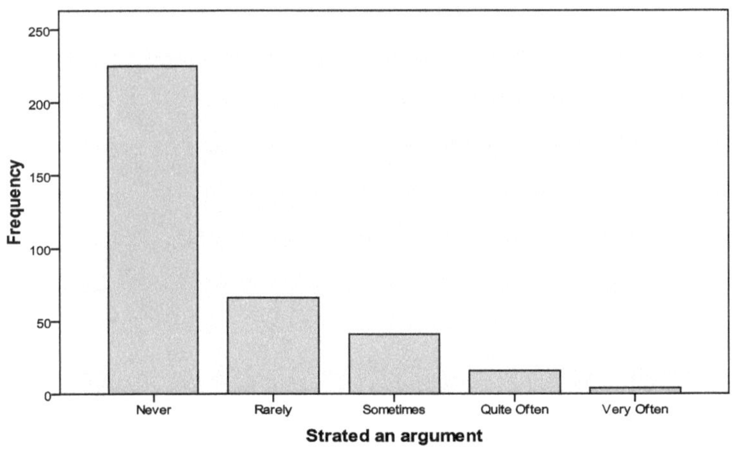

Verbally abused someone

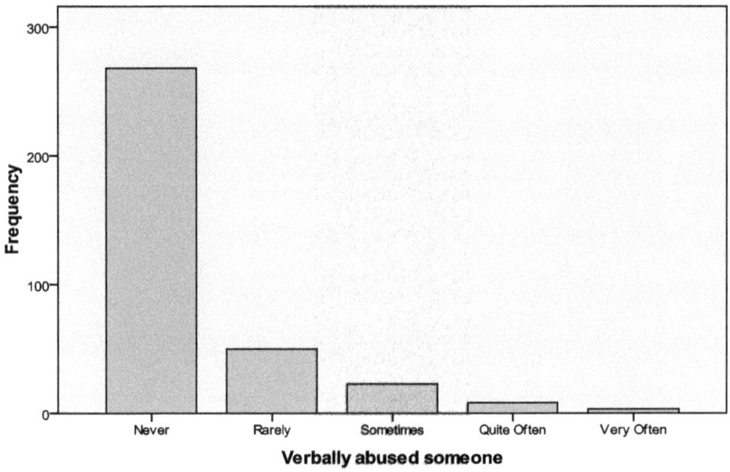

Threatned someone

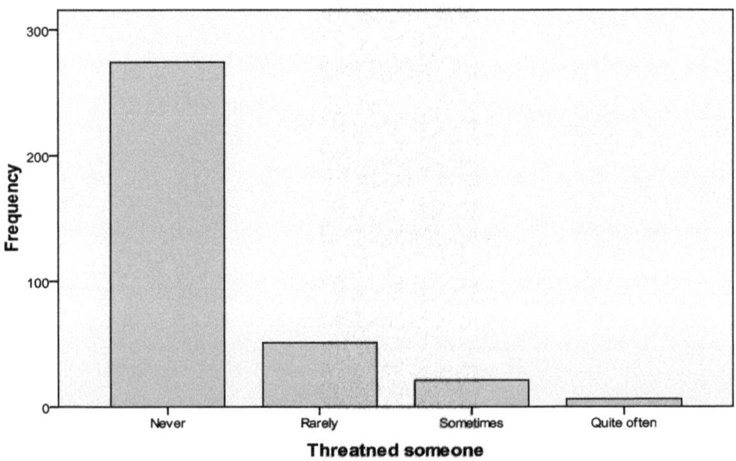

Said something to others

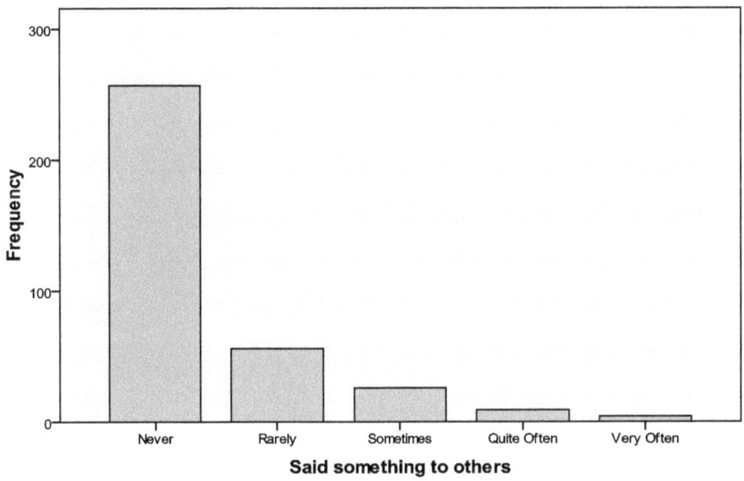

Looked at someone's private mails

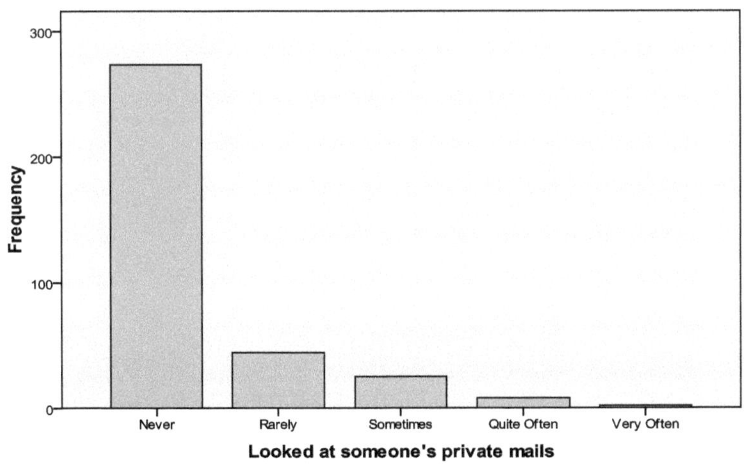

Hit or pushed someone

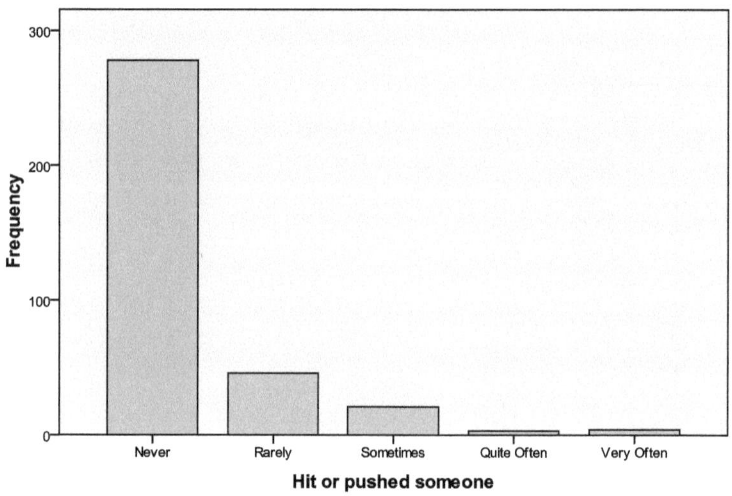

Insulted or made fun of someone

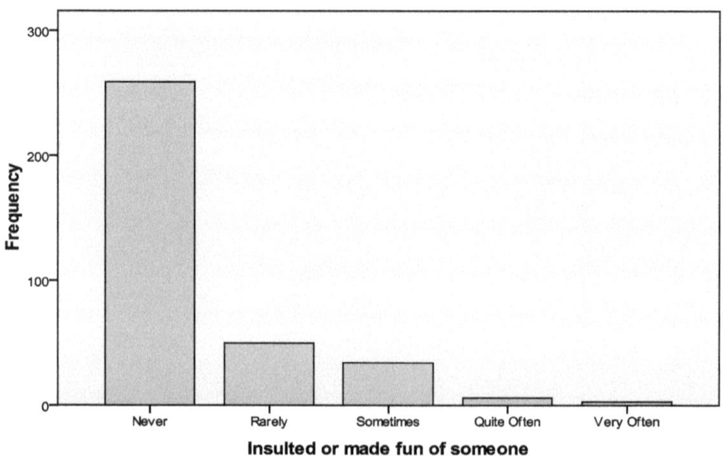

Appendix B

Frequency and percentage tables of demographics

Gender

	Frequency	Percent	Cumulative Percent
Male	276	78.4	78.4
Female	76	21.6	100.0
Total	352	100.0	

Age

	Frequency	Percent	Cumulative Percent
Under 26	67	19.0	19.0
26-35	126	35.8	54.8
36-45	92	26.1	81.0
46-55	46	13.1	94.0
56+	21	6.0	100.0
Total	352	100.0	

Monthly Salary

	Frequency	Percent	Cumulative Percent
Less than 25,000	76	21.6	21.6
25,000-40,000	128	36.4	58.0
40,001-55,000	75	21.3	79.3
55,001-70,000	41	11.6	90.9
More than 70,000	32	9.1	100.0
Total	352	100.0	

Doing this job for

	Frequency	Percent	Cumulative Percent
Few months less than 1 year	33	9.4	9.4
1-3 years	80	22.7	32.1
3-6 years	85	24.1	56.3
6-9 years	53	15.1	71.3
More than 9 years	101	28.7	100.0
Total	352	100.0	

Nature of job

	Frequency	Percent	Cumulative Percent
You have to work in this office	242	68.8	68.8
You have a field job	30	8.5	77.3
Both office and field job	80	22.7	100.0
Total	352	100.0	

Total professional experience

	Frequency	Percent	Cumulative Percent
Few months less than 1 year	25	7.1	7.1
1-3 years	74	21.0	28.1
3-6 years	75	21.3	49.4
6-9 years	46	13.1	62.5
More than 9 years	132	37.5	100.0
Total	352	100.0	

Jobs switched

	Frequency	Percent	Cumulative Percent
No its my first job	195	55.4	55.4
Less than 2	118	33.5	88.9
Less than 4	26	7.4	96.3
Less than 6	5	1.4	97.7
More than 6	8	2.3	100.0
Total	352	100.0	

Time to reach office

	Frequency	Percent	Cumulative Percent
Less than 10 minutes	40	11.4	11.4
10-20 minutes	138	39.2	50.6
21-40 minutes	124	35.2	85.8
41-60 minutes	38	10.8	96.6
More than an hour	12	3.4	100.0
Total	352	100.0	

Nature of family

	Frequency	Percent	Cumulative Percent
Joint family	257	73.0	73.0
Nuclear family	95	27.0	100.0
Total	352	100.0	

House in which live in

	Frequency	Percent	Cumulative Percent
Your own house	243	69.0	69.0
Rented house	95	27.0	96.0
Leased house	14	4.0	100.0
Total	352	100.0	

Type of conveyance

	Frequency	Percent	Cumulative Percent
Persoanl (car or bike)	270	76.7	76.7
Ofiicial	17	4.8	81.5
Auto	21	6.0	87.5
Bus	39	11.1	98.6
Any other	5	1.4	100.0
Total	352	100.0	

No of children

	Frequency	Percent	Cumulative Percent
No one	157	44.6	44.6
Less than 2	123	34.9	79.5
3-4	64	18.2	97.7
5-6	7	2.0	99.7
More than 6	1	.3	100.0
Total	352	100.0	

Designation in bank

	Frequency	Percent	Cumulative Percent
AVP	70	19.9	19.9
OG-I	97	27.6	47.4
OG-II	95	27.0	74.4
OG-III	90	25.6	100.0
Total	352	100.0	

Educational level attained

	Frequency	Percent	Cumulative Percent
High school diploma	8	2.3	2.3
Bachelors degree	165	46.9	49.1
Master's degree	175	49.7	98.9
Doctorate	4	1.1	100.0
Total	352	100.0	

Marital status

	Frequency	Percent	Cumulative Percent
Single	126	35.8	35.8
Married	211	59.9	95.7
Separated	7	2.0	97.7
Divorced	7	2.0	99.7
Widowed	1	.3	100.0
Total	352	100.0	

Comfortable using computers

	Frequency	Percent	Cumulative Percent
Very comfortable	176	50.0	50.0
Somewhat comfortable	92	26.1	76.1
Neither comfortable nor uncomfortable	45	12.8	88.9
Somewhat uncomfortable	28	8.0	96.9
Very Uncomfortable	11	3.1	100.0
Total	352	100.0	

satisfied with internet skills

	Frequency	Percent	Cumulative Percent
Very satisfied	160	45.5	45.5
somewhat satisfied	112	31.8	77.3
Neither satisfied nor unsatisfied	46	13.1	90.3
Somewhat unsatisfied	21	6.0	96.3
Very unsatisfied	13	3.7	100.0
Total	352	100.0	

Frequency tables of Job Stress

Huge deal of attention

	Frequency	Percent	Cumulative Percent
Strongly Disagree	7	2.0	2.0
Disagree	32	9.1	11.1
Neutral	46	13.1	24.1
Agree	203	57.7	81.8
Strongly Agree	64	18.2	100.0
Total	352	100.0	

Remember different things

	Frequency	Percent	Cumulative Percent
Strongly Disagree	9	2.6	2.6
Disagree	43	12.2	14.8
Neutral	50	14.2	29.0
Agree	166	47.2	76.1
Strongly Agree	84	23.9	100.0
Total	352	100.0	

excessive workload than normal

	Frequency	Percent	Cumulative Percent
Strongly Disagree	11	3.1	3.1
Disagree	70	19.9	23.0
Neutral	82	23.3	46.3
Agree	136	38.6	84.9
Strongly Agree	53	15.1	100.0
Total	352	100.0	

Could not finish work in work day

	Frequency	Percent	Cumulative Percent
Strongly Disagree	20	5.7	5.7
Disagree	113	32.1	37.8
Neutral	67	19.0	56.8
Agree	99	28.1	84.9
Strongly Agree	53	15.1	100.0
Total	352	100.0	

Forced to work more

	Frequency	Percent	Cumulative Percent
Strongly Disagree	35	9.9	9.9
Disagree	88	25.0	34.9
Neutral	82	23.3	58.2
Agree	110	31.3	89.5
Strongly Agree	36	10.2	99.7
Total	352	100.0	

Poor communication

	Frequency	Percent	Cumulative Percent
Strongly Disagree	62	17.6	17.6
Disagree	100	28.4	46.0
Neutral	68	19.3	65.3
Agree	94	26.7	92.0
Strongly Agree	28	8.0	100.0
Total	352	100.0	

Unclear responsibilities and roles

	Frequency	Percent	Cumulative Percent
Strongly Disag-ree	78	22.2	22.2
Disagree	128	36.4	58.5
Neutral	66	18.8	77.3
Agree	60	17.0	94.3
Strongly Agree	20	5.7	100.0
Total	352	100.0	

Conflicts in staff members

	Frequency	Percent	Cumulative Percent
Strongly Disag-ree	67	19.0	19.0
Disagree	106	30.1	49.1
Neutral	68	19.3	68.5
Agree	87	24.7	93.2
Strongly Agree	24	6.8	100.0
Total	352	100.0	

Not receive any appreciation

	Frequency	Percent	Cumulative Percent
Strongly Disag-ree	38	10.8	10.8
Disagree	111	31.5	42.3
Neutral	74	21.0	63.4
Agree	100	28.4	91.8
Strongly Agree	29	8.2	100.0
Total	352	100.0	

Unfair performance evaluation system

	Frequency	Percent	Cumulative Percent
Strongly Disag-ree	34	9.7	9.7
Disagree	118	33.5	43.2
Neutral	80	22.7	65.9
Agree	88	25.0	90.9
Strongly Agree	32	9.1	100.0
Total	352	100.0	

No opportunities for advancement

	Frequency	Percent	Cumulative Percent
Strongly disag-ree	44	12.5	12.5
Disagree	128	36.4	48.9
Neutral	77	21.9	70.7
Agree	84	23.9	94.6
Strongly Agree	19	5.4	100.0
Total	352	100.0	

Technological problems

		Frequency	Percent	Cumulative Percent
	Strongly Disag-ree	73	20.7	20.8
	Disagree	135	38.4	59.3
	Neutral	58	16.5	75.8
	Agree	72	20.5	96.3
	Strongly Agree	13	3.7	100.0
	Total	351	99.7	
Missing	**System**	1	.3	
Total		352	100.0	

Age problems

		Frequency	Percent	Cumulative Percent
	Strongly Disag-ree	81	23.0	23.0
	Disagree	149	42.3	65.3
	Neutral	45	12.8	78.1
	Agree	62	17.6	95.7
	Strongly Agree	15	4.3	100.0
	Total	352	100.0	

Level of noise in working area

	Frequency	Percent	Cumulative Percent
Strongly Disagree	36	10.2	10.2
Disagree	127	36.1	46.3
Neutral	73	20.7	67.0
Agree	91	25.9	92.9
Strongly Agree	25	7.1	100.0
Total	352	100.0	

Extremely crowded area

	Frequency	Percent	Cumulative Percent
Strongly Disagree	33	9.4	9.4
Disagree	122	34.7	44.0
Neutral	74	21.0	65.1
Agree	103	29.3	94.3
Strongly Agree	20	5.7	100.0
Total	352	100.0	

Pressure of boss to work more

	Frequency	Percent	Cumulative Percent
Strongly Disagree	45	12.8	12.8
Disagree	150	42.6	55.4
Neutral	70	19.9	75.3
Agree	73	20.7	96.0
Strongly Agree	14	4.0	100.0
Total	352	100.0	

No emotional attachment to work

	Frequency	Percent	Cumulative Percent
Strongly Disag-ree	47	13.4	13.4
Disagree	125	35.5	48.9
Neutral	71	20.2	69.0
Agree	90	25.6	94.6
Strongly Agree	19	5.4	100.0
Total	352	100.0	

Bundle of tasks

	Frequency	Percent	Cumulative Percent
Strongly Disag-ree	36	10.2	10.2
Disagree	120	34.1	44.3
Neutral	87	24.7	69.0
Agree	94	26.7	95.7
Strongly Agree	15	4.3	100.0
Total	352	100.0	

Boss shouting

	Frequency	Percent	Cumulative Percent
Strongly Disagree	89	25.3	25.3
Disagree	144	40.9	66.2
Neutral	57	16.2	82.4
Agree	51	14.5	96.9
Strongly Agree	11	3.1	100.0
Total	352	100.0	

Leg pullying behavior of colleagues

	Frequency	Percent	Cumulative Percent
Strongly Disagree	54	15.3	15.3
Disagree	126	35.8	51.1
Neutral	90	25.6	76.7
Agree	68	19.3	96.0
Strongly Agree	14	4.0	100.0
Total	352	100.0	

Uncomfortable workplace

	Frequency	Percent	Cumulative Percent
Strongly Disagree	72	20.5	20.5
Disgaree	144	40.9	61.4
Neutral	64	18.2	79.5
Agree	54	15.3	94.9
Strongly Agree	18	5.1	100.0
Total	352	100.0	

Unsatisfied with salary and rewards

	Frequency	Percent	Cumulative Percent
Strongly Disag-ree	46	13.1	13.1
Disagree	109	31.0	44.0
Neutral	66	18.8	62.8
Agree	92	26.1	88.9
Strongly Agree	39	11.1	100.0
Total	352	100.0	

Long working hours

	Frequency	Percent	Cumulative Percent
Strongly Disag-ree	46	13.1	13.1
Disagree	120	34.1	47.2
Neutral	83	23.6	70.7
Agree	79	22.4	93.2
Strongly Agree	24	6.8	100.0
Total	352	100.0	

Boring and dull workplace

	Frequency	Percent	Cumulative Percent
Strongly Disagree	69	19.6	19.6
Disagree	137	38.9	58.5
Neutral	72	20.5	79.0
Agree	56	15.9	94.9
Strongly Agree	18	5.1	100.0
Total	352	100.0	

Frequency tables of CWB

Purposely wasted materials/supplies

	Frequency	Percent	Cumulative Percent
Never	117	33.2	33.2
Rarely	126	35.8	69.0
Sometimes	60	17.0	86.1
Quite Often	30	8.5	94.6
Very Often	19	5.4	100.0
Total	352	100.0	

Purposely damaged equipment/property

	Frequency	Percent	Cumulative Percent
Never	126	35.8	35.8
Rarely	114	32.4	68.2
Sometimes	59	16.8	84.9
Quite Often	36	10.2	95.2
Very Often	17	4.8	100.0
Total	352	100.0	

Purposely dirtied/littered workplace

	Frequency	Percent	Cumulative Percent
Never	118	33.5	33.5
Rarely	115	32.7	66.2
Sometimes	70	19.9	86.1
Quite Often	31	8.8	94.9
Very Often	18	5.1	100.0
Total	352	100.0	

Come to work late withour permission

	Frequency	Percent	Cumulative Percent
Never	123	34.9	34.9
Rarely	104	29.5	64.5
Sometimes	66	18.8	83.2
Quite Often	33	9.4	92.6
Very Often	26	7.4	100.0
Total	352	100.0	

Stayed home to avoid home

	Frequency	Percent	Cumulative Percent
Never	148	42.0	42.0
Rarely	90	25.6	67.6
Sometimes	64	18.2	85.8
Quite Often	24	6.8	92.6
Very Often	26	7.4	100.0
Total	352	100.0	

Taken a longer break

	Frequency	Percent	Cumulative Percent
Never	145	41.2	41.2
Rarely	79	22.4	63.6
Sometimes	81	23.0	86.6
Quite Often	29	8.2	94.9
Very Often	18	5.1	100.0
Total	352	100.0	

Left work earlier than allowed

	Frequency	Percent	Cumulative Percent
Never	165	46.9	46.9
Rarely	77	21.9	68.8
Sometimes	73	20.7	89.5
Quite Ofetn	18	5.1	94.6
Very Often	19	5.4	100.0
Total	352	100.0	

Purposely did the work incorrectly

	Frequency	Percent	Cumulative Percent
Never	203	57.7	57.7
Rarely	62	17.6	75.3
Sometimes	54	15.3	90.6
Quite Often	16	4.5	95.2
Very Often	17	4.8	100.0
Total	352	100.0	

Purposely worked slowly

	Frequency	Percent	Cumulative Percent
Never	193	54.8	54.8
Rarely	76	21.6	76.4
Sometimes	56	15.9	92.3
Quite Often	15	4.3	96.6
Very Often	12	3.4	100.0
Total	352	100.0	

Purposely don't follow instructions

	Frequency	Percent	Cumulative Percent
Never	201	57.1	57.1
Rarely	81	23.0	80.1
Sometimes	49	13.9	94.0
Quite Often	13	3.7	97.7
Very Often	8	2.3	100.0
Total	352	100.0	

Stole something of colleagues

	Frequency	Percent	Cumulative Percent
Never	240	68.2	68.2
Rarely	56	15.9	84.1
Sometimes	39	11.1	95.2
Quite Often	14	4.0	99.1
Very Often	3	.9	100.0
Total	352	100.0	

Took supplies home without permission

	Frequency	Percent	Cumulative Percent
Never	234	66.5	66.5
Rarely	51	14.5	81.0
Sometimes	51	14.5	95.5
Quite Often	12	3.4	98.9
Very Often	4	1.1	100.0
Total	352	100.0	

Put in to be paid for more hours

	Frequency	Percent	Cumulative Percent
Never	239	67.9	67.9
Rarely	61	17.3	85.2
Sometimes	37	10.5	95.7
Quite Often	8	2.3	98.0
Very Often	7	2.0	100.0
Total	352	100.0	

Took money of your employer

	Frequency	Percent	Cumulative Percent
Never	263	74.7	74.7
Rarely	44	12.5	87.2
Sometimes	32	9.1	96.3
Quite Often	9	2.6	98.9
Very Often	4	1.1	100.0
Total	352	100.0	

Stole something of someone

	Frequency	Percent	Cumulative Percent
Never	262	74.4	74.4
Rarely	50	14.2	88.6
Sometimes	29	8.2	96.9
Quite Often	8	2.3	99.1
Very Often	3	.9	100.0
Total	352	100.0	

Been nasty or rude to customers

	Frequency	Percent	Cumulative Percent
Never	242	68.8	68.8
Rarely	61	17.3	86.1
Sometimes	33	9.4	95.5
Quite Often	11	3.1	98.6
Very Often	5	1.4	100.0
Total	352	100.0	

Insulted someone

	Frequency	Percent	Cumulative Percent
Never	242	68.8	68.8
Rarely	58	16.5	85.2
Sometimes	32	9.1	94.3
Quite Often	17	4.8	99.1
Very Often	3	.9	100.0
Total	352	100.0	

Fun of someone's personal life

	Frequency	Percent	Cumulative Percent
Never	231	65.6	65.6
Rarely	68	19.3	84.9
Sometimes	41	11.6	96.6
Quite Often	11	3.1	99.7
Very Often	1	.3	100.0
Total	352	100.0	

Ignored someone at work

	Frequency	Percent	Cumulative Percent
Never	230	65.3	65.3
Rarely	65	18.5	83.8
Sometimes	43	12.2	96.0
Quite Often	12	3.4	99.4
Very Often	2	.6	100.0
Total	352	100.0	

Blamed someone for error you made

	Frequency	Percent	Cumulative Percent
Never	246	69.9	69.9
Rarely	56	15.9	85.8
Sometimes	30	8.5	94.3
Quite Often	16	4.5	98.9
Very Often	4	1.1	100.0
Total	352	100.0	

Started an argument

	Frequency	Percent	Cumulative Percent
Never	225	63.9	63.9
Rarely	66	18.8	82.7
Sometimes	41	11.6	94.3
Quite Often	16	4.5	98.9
Very Often	4	1.1	100.0
Total	352	100.0	

Verbally abused someone

	Frequency	Percent	Cumulative Percent
Never	268	76.1	76.1
Rarely	50	14.2	90.3
Sometimes	23	6.5	96.9
Quite Often	8	2.3	99.1
Very Often	3	.9	100.0
Total	352	100.0	

Threatened someone

	Frequency	Percent	Cumulative Percent
Never	274	77.8	77.8
Rarely	51	14.5	92.3
Sometimes	21	6.0	98.3
Quite often	6	1.7	100.0
Total	352	100.0	

Threatened someone but not physically

	Frequency	Percent	Cumulative Percent
Never	274	77.8	77.8
Rarely	54	15.3	93.2
Sometimes	16	4.5	97.7
Quite Often	5	1.4	99.1
Very Often	3	.9	100.0
Total	352	100.0	

Said something to others

	Frequency	Percent	Cumulative Percent
Never	257	73.0	73.0
Rarely	56	15.9	88.9
Sometimes	26	7.4	96.3
Quite Often	9	2.6	98.9
Very Often	4	1.1	100.0
Total	352	100.0	

Looked at someone's private mails

	Frequency	Percent	Cumulative Percent
Never	273	77.6	77.6
Rarely	44	12.5	90.1
Sometimes	25	7.1	97.2
Quite Often	8	2.3	99.4
Very Often	2	.6	100.0
Total	352	100.0	

Hit or pushed someone

	Frequency	Percent	Cumulative Percent
Never	278	79.0	79.0
Rarely	46	13.1	92.0
Sometimes	21	6.0	98.0
Quite Often	3	.9	98.9
Very Often	4	1.1	100.0
Total	352	100.0	

Insulted or made fun of someone

	Frequency	Percent
Never	259	73.6
Rarely	50	14.2
Sometimes	34	9.7
Quite Often	6	1.7
Very Often	3	.9
Total	352	100.0

Appendix C

Advanced Statistical Tests

Reliability Test

Reliability test of Work Stress

Reliability Statistics

Cronbach's Alpha	N of Items
.938	25

Reliability test of CWB

Reliability Statistics

Cronbach's Alpha	N of Items
.963	28

Reliability test of questionnaire

Reliability Statistics

Cronbach's Alpha	N of Items
.942	71

Mann Whitney Test

Ranks

	Gender	N	Mean Rank	Sum of Ranks
Variable 1: Job Stress	Male	276	176.25	48645.50
	Female	76	177.40	13482.50
	Total	352		
Variable 2: CWB	Male	276	182.03	50241.50
	Female	76	156.40	11886.50
	Total	352		

Test Statistics

	Variable 1: Job Stress	Variable 2: CWB
Mann-Whitney U	10419.500	8960.500
Wilcoxon W	48645.500	11886.500
Z	-.087	-1.946
Asymp. Sig. (2-tailed)	.931	.052

a. Grouping Variable: Gender

Ranks

	Nature of family	N	Mean Rank	Sum of Ranks
Variable 1: Job Stress	Joint family	257	186.00	47803.00
	Nuclear family	95	150.79	14325.00
	Total	352		
Variable 2: CWB	Joint family	257	180.41	46366.50
	Nuclear family	95	165.91	15761.50
	Total	352		

Test Statistics[a]

	Variable 1: Job Stress	Variable 2: CWB
Mann-Whitney U	9765.000	11201.500
Wilcoxon W	14325.000	15761.500
Z	-2.882	-1.188
Asymp. Sig. (2-tailed)	.004	.235

a. Grouping Variable: Nature of family

ANOVA

Time to reach office

ANOVA

		Sum of Squares	df	Mean Square	F	Sig.
Variable 1: Job Stress	Between Groups	5.434	4	1.358	2.312	.057
	Within Groups	203.915	347	.588		
	Total	209.348	351			
Variable 2: CWB	Between Groups	6.330	4	1.582	3.036	.018
	Within Groups	180.867	347	.521		
	Total	187.197	351			

Education level

ANOVA

		Sum of Squares	df	Mean Square	F	Sig.
Variable 1: Job Stress	Between Groups	.605	3	.202	.336	.799
	Within Groups	208.743	348	.600		
	Total	209.348	351			
Variable 2: CWB	Between Groups	.853	3	.284	.531	.661
	Within Groups	186.344	348	.535		
	Total	187.197	351			

Kruskal Wallis Test

Age

	Variable 1: Job Stress	Variable 2: CWB
Chi-Square	6.986	21.571
df	4	4
Asymp. Sig.	.137	.000

a. Kruskal Wallis Test

b. Grouping Variable: Age

Monthly Salary[b]

	Variable 1: Job Stress	Variable 2: CWB
Chi-Square	4.856	10.579
df	4	4
Asymp. Sig.	.302	.032

a. Kruskal Wallis Test

b. Grouping Variable: Monthly Salary

Doing this job for

	Variable 1: Job Stress	Variable 2: CWB
Chi-Square	10.397	13.015
df	4	4
Asymp. Sig.	.034	.011

a. Kruskal Wallis Test

b. Grouping Variable: Doing this job for

Nature of job

	Variable 1: Job Stress	Variable 2: CWB
Chi-Square	.645	14.300
df	2	2
Asymp. Sig.	.724	.001

a. Kruskal Wallis Test

b. Grouping Variable: Nature of job

Total Professional Experience

	Variable 1: Job Stress	Variable 2: CWB
Chi-Square	6.493	6.577
df	4	4
Asymp. Sig.	.165	.160

a. Kruskal Wallis Test

b. Grouping Variable: Total professional experience

Jobs Switched

	Variable 1: Job Stress	Variable 2: CWB
Chi-Square	11.103	3.334
df	4	4
Asymp. Sig.	.025	.503

a. Kruskal Wallis Test

b. Grouping Variable: Jobs switched

Type of House

	Variable 1: Job Stress	Variable 2: CWB
Chi-Square	1.796	2.962
df	2	2
Asymp. Sig.	.407	.227

a. Kruskal Wallis Test

b. Grouping Variable: House in which live in

Type of Conveyance

	Variable 1: Job Stress	Variable 2: CWB
Chi-Square	4.241	4.252
df	4	4
Asymp. Sig.	.374	.373

a. Kruskal Wallis Test

b. Grouping Variable: Type of conveyance

No. of dependents

	Variable 1: Job Stress	Variable 2: CWB
Chi-Square	6.308	14.792
df	4	4
Asymp. Sig.	.177	.005

a. Kruskal Wallis Test

b. Grouping Variable: No of dependents

Designation

	Variable 1: Job Stress	Variable 2: CWB
Chi-Square	6.674	4.271
df	3	3
Asymp. Sig.	.083	.234

a. Kruskal Wallis Test

b. Grouping Variable: Designation in bank

Marital Status

	Variable 1: Job Stress	Variable 2: CWB
Chi-Square	4.232	6.059
df	4	4
Asymp. Sig.	.376	.195

a. Kruskal Wallis Test

b. Grouping Variable: Marital status

Comfortable using computers

	Variable 1: Job Stress	Variable 2: CWB
Chi-Square	20.280	37.960
df	4	4
Asymp. Sig.	.000	.000

a. Kruskal Wallis Test

b. Grouping Variable: Comfortable using computers

Satisfied with internet skills

	Variable 1: Job Stress	Variable 2: CWB
Chi-Square	8.860	19.786
df	4	4
Asymp. Sig.	.065	.001

a. Kruskal Wallis Test

b. Grouping Variable: satisfied with internet skills

Correlation Analysis

Correlations

		Variable 1: Job Stress	Variable 2: CWB
Variable 1: Job Stress	Pearson Correlation	1	.379**
	Sig. (2-tailed)		.000
	N	352	352
Variable 2: CWB	Pearson Correlation	.379**	1
	Sig. (2-tailed)	.000	
	N	352	352

**. Correlation is significant at the 0.01 level (2-tailed).

Regression Analysis

Model Summary

Model	R	R Square	Adjusted R Square	Std. Error of the Estimate
1	.379[a]	.144	.141	.67669

a. Predictors: (Constant), Variable 1: Job Stress

Coefficients[a]

Model		Unstandardized Coefficients		Standardized Coefficients	t	Sig.
		B	Std. Error	Beta		
1	(Constant)	.747	.136		5.473	.000
	Variable 1: Job Stress	.359	.047	.379	7.668	.000

a. Dependent Variable: Variable 2: CWB

Appendix D

Questionnaire

PERSONAL INFORMATION

Background details

		Please Circle
1. Are you:	Male	1
	Female	2
2. Age:	Under 26	1
	26-35	2
	36-45	3
	46-55	4
	56+	5
3. Monthly Salary	Less than 25,000	1
	25,000-40,000	2
	40,001-55,000	3
	55,001-70,000	4
	More than 70,000	5
4. Doing this job for	Few months less than 1 year	1
	1 year to 3 years	2
	3 years to 6 years	3
	6 years to 9 years	4
	More than 9 years	5
5. Nature of your job	You have to work in office	1
	You have a field job	2
	Both office and field job	3
6. Total period of professional experience		
	Few months less than 1 year	1
	1 year to 3 years	2
	3 years to 6 years	3
	6 years to 9 years	4
	More than 9 years	5

7. No of jobs you have switched

	No it's my first job	1
	Less than 2	2
	Less than 4	3
	Less than 6	4
	More than 6	5

8. Time to reach your office from your house is		**Please circle**
	Less than 10 minutes	1
	10-20 minutes	2
	21-40 minutes	3
	41-60 minutes	4
	More than an hour	5

9. Nature of your Family

	Joint Family	1
	Nuclear Family	2

10. You live in	Your own house	1
	Rented House	2
	Leased house	3

11. Type of conveyance you are using

	Personal (car or bike)	1
	Official	2
	Auto	3
	Bus	4
	Any other	5

12. No of dependents

	No one	1
	Less than 3	2
	3 - 5	3
	5-8	4
	More than 8	5

13. No of Children

	No one	1
	Less than 2	2
	3 - 4	3
	5 - 6	4
	More than 6	5

14. Designation in bank

AVP	1
OG-I	2
OG-II	3
OG-III	4

15. What education level have you attained so far?

High school diploma	1
Bachelor's degree	2
Master's degree	3
Doctorate	4

16. What is your current marital status?

Single, never married	1
Married	2
Separated	3
Divorced	4
Widowed	5

17. How comfortable do you feel using computers, in general?

	Please circle
Very comfortable	1
Somewhat comfortable	2
Neither comfortable nor uncomfortable	3
Somewhat uncomfortable	4
Very uncomfortable	5

18. How satisfied are you with your current skills for using the Internet?

Very satisfied - I can do everything that I want to do	1
Somewhat satisfied - I can do most things I want to do	2
Neither satisfied nor unsatisfied	3
Somewhat unsatisfied - I can't do many things I want to do	4
Very unsatisfied - I can't do most things I would like to do	5

	Do you agree with these kinds of feelings?	**Strongly Disagree Disagree Neutral**
1.	My job requires huge deal of attention beyond my job's range.	1 2 3 4 5
2.	My job requires me to remember many different things.	1 2 3 4 5
3.	I have excessive workload than normal work.	1 2 3 4 5
4.	Due to excessive workload, I could not finish my work during the normal work day.	1 2 3 4 5
5.	Most of the time I am forced to work more.	1 2 3 4 5

6.	There is a poor communication between my staff members and different departments.	1	2	3	4	5
7.	My job responsibilities and role in the organization are not clear.	1	2	3	4	5
8.	There are conflicts between staff members.	1	2	3	4	5
9.	I do not receive any appreciation when my work is really good.	1	2	3	4	5
10.	There is unfair performance evaluation system in our organization.	1	2	3	4	5
11.	There are no opportunities of advancement in my organization.	1	2	3	4	5
12.	Due to technological change, it is difficult for me to deal with problems.	1	2	3	4	5
13.	Due to age factor, it is not easy for me to cope with changes.	1	2	3	4	5
14.	The level of noise in the area in which I work is high.	1	2	3	4	5
15.	My work area is extremely crowded.	1	2	3	4	5
16.	My boss pressurizes me to work more than what I am assigned to do	1	2	3	4	5
17.	I don't feel any kind of emotional attachment with my work	1	2	3	4	5
18.	Always there is a bundle of tasks for me to be undertaken	1	2	3	4	5
19.	My boss shouts at me	1	2	3	4	5
20.	I experience leg pulling behavior from my colleagues	1	2	3	4	5
21.	I have uncomfortable workplace	1	2	3	4	5
22.	I am not satisfied with my salary and rewards this is not what I deserve	1	2	3	4	5
23.	At my work place there are long working hours	1	2	3	4	5
24.	My work place is Boring and dull.	1	2	3	4	5
25.	There is so much pressure of work that I have to work overtime even on the weekends	1	2	3	4	5

	How often have you done each of the following things on your present job only **when you are stressed because of work**?	**Rarely**	**Sometime**	**Quite often**	**Very Of-**	
1.	Purposely wasted materials/supplies available in my organization	1	2	3	4	5
2.	Purposely damaged equipment or property of my organization	1	2	3	4	5
3.	Purposely dirtied or littered your place of work	1	2	3	4	5
4.	Came to work late without permission	1	2	3	4	5
5.	Stayed home to avoid work and said you were sick when you weren't	1	2	3	4	5
6.	Taken a longer break than you were allowed to take	1	2	3	4	5
7.	Left work earlier than you were allowed to	1	2	3	4	5
8.	Purposely did the work assigned to you incorrectly	1	2	3	4	5
9.	Purposely worked slowly when things needed to get done	1	2	3	4	5
10.	Purposely don't follow the instructions	1	2	3	4	5
11.	Stolen something belonging to your colleagues at work	1	2	3	4	5
12.	Took supplies or tools home without permission	1	2	3	4	5

13.	Put in to be paid for more hours than you worked	1 2 3 4 5
14.	Took money from your employer without permission	1 2 3 4 5
15.	Stole something belonging to someone at work	1 2 3 4 5
16.	Been nasty or rude to a client or customer	1 2 3 4 5
17.	Insulted someone about their job performance	1 2 3 4 5
18.	Made fun of someone's personal life	1 2 3 4 5
19.	Ignored someone at work	1 2 3 4 5
20.	Blamed someone at work for error you made	1 2 3 4 5
21.	Started an argument with someone at work	1 2 3 4 5
22.	Verbally abused someone at work	1 2 3 4 5
23.	Threatened someone at work with violence	1 2 3 4 5
24.	Threatened someone at work, but not physically	1 2 3 4 5
25.	Said something to someone at work to make them feel bad	1 2 3 4 5
26.	Looked at someone at work's private mail/property without permission	1 2 3 4 5
27.	Hit or pushed someone at work	1 2 3 4 5
28.	Insulted or made fun of someone at work	1 2 3 4 5